Introducing the Theory of Computation

Wayne Goddard
Clemson University

JONES AND BARTLETT PUBLISHERS
Sudbury, Massachusetts
BOSTON   TORONTO   LONDON   SINGAPORE

World Headquarters

Jones and Bartlett Publishers
40 Tall Pine Drive
Sudbury, MA 01776
978-443-5000
info@jbpub.com
www.jbpub.com

Jones and Bartlett Publishers
Canada
6339 Ormindale Way
Mississauga, Ontario L5V 1J2
Canada

Jones and Bartlett Publishers
International
Barb House, Barb Mews
London W6 7PA
United Kingdom

Jones and Bartlett's books and products are available through most bookstores and online booksellers. To contact Jones and Bartlett Publishers directly, call 800-832-0034, fax 978-443-8000, or visit our website www.jbpub.com.

Substantial discounts on bulk quantities of Jones and Bartlett's publications are available to corporations, professional associations, and other qualified organizations. For details and specific discount information, contact the special sales department at Jones and Bartlett via the above contact information or send an email to specialsales@jbpub.com.

Production Credits
Acquisitions Editor: Tim Anderson
Production Director: Amy Rose
Editorial Assistant: Melissa Elmore
Senior Marketing Manager: Andrea DeFronzo
Manufacturing Buyer: Therese Connell
Composition: Northeast Compositors
Cover Design: Kate Ternullo
Cover Image: © Cindy Hughes/ShutterStock, Inc. and © Andreas Nilsson/ShutterStock, Inc.
Printing and Binding: Malloy, Inc.
Cover Printing: Malloy, Inc.

Library of Congress Cataloging-in-Publication Data
Goddard, Wayne.
  Introducing the theory of computation / Wayne Goddard. — 1st ed.
     p. cm.
  Includes bibliographical references and index.
  ISBN-13: 978-0-7637-4125-9
  ISBN-10: 0-7637-4125-6
  1. Machine theory. 2. Computational complexity. I. Title.
  QA267.G57 2008
  511.3'5—dc22
                          2007049462

6048
Printed in the United States of America
12   10 9 8 7 6 5 4 3 2

To Stuart, friend and collaborator forever

Preface

Instructions for using this book: Read, think, repeat.

To the Instructor

This is a text for an undergraduate course in the theory of computation; it is also appropriate for courses in automata theory and formal languages. The text covers the standard three models of finite automata, grammars, and Turing machines, as well as undecidability. An introduction to time and space complexity theories and a separate part on the basics of complexity theory are also included.

Goals and Features

When I wrote this text, I focused on the standard material for a course in the theory of computation or automata theory. As a result, this text provides a concise introduction to core topics taught in a course on either of these subjects.

One difference between this text and others on the subject is the use of flowcharts for the pushdown automata. Another difference is that although the material is undoubtedly mathematical, I have tried to reduce the use of mathematical notation. Additionally, this text incorporates the following:

- an engaging, student-friendly writing style that moves through material at a pace appropriate for undergraduate students
- a wide range of problems, varying in level of difficulty, which allows students to test themselves on key material covered in the given chapter

Solutions to selected exercises are in the appendix and are noted with the symbol ★. The most difficult exercises are labeled with the symbol ⓗ.

Full solutions are provided in the Online Instructor's Manual, which is available online through the Jones and Bartlett website at: http://www.jbpub.com/catalog/9780763741259/.

Organization

The text is divided into five parts: Regular Languages, Context-Free Languages, Turing Machines, Undecidability, and Complexity Theory. The final chapter in each of the five parts can be viewed as optional—specifically, Chapters 5, 10, 16, and 19. These chapters provide additional information but can be omitted without any impact on the overall course. I include more material than necessary for a single semester course, which provides instructors with the freedom to structure their course and omit or include whichever relevant topics they choose.

To the Student

Welcome to the theory of computation! The material is theoretical, although the early stages are less so. Part IV, Undecidability, is both theoretical and challenging.

As you work through the text, do not lose yourself in the theoretical details. Remember the bigger picture! The finite automata and grammars we see in the first few parts are two of the most efficient and successful techniques in computer programming. The Turing machines and later material show that there are limits to what computer programming can do, even if the actual boundaries are not yet clear. There are problems, procedures, programs, and paradoxes. I encourage you to read and re-read the more difficult sections for better understanding.

The exercises are at varied levels of difficulty. Exercises that are more challenging are marked with the symbol ⓗ. Solutions to problems marked with the symbol ★ are provided in the appendix.

Acknowledgments

I was very fortunate to have many people help me write and publish this text. Thank you to my professor at MIT, Michael Sipser, for his instruction. Thanks to family and friends, past and present. In particular, thanks go to Steve Hedetniemi for offering some of his problems and to my students at Clemson University who class-tested early drafts of the text.

Thanks also to the readers and reviewers whose comments greatly improved the book:

Petros Drineas, Rensselaer Polytechnic Institute
Stephen T. Hedetniemi, Clemson University
K. N. King, Georgia State University
Anne-Louise Radimsky, California State University, Sacramento
Neil W. Rickert, Northern Illinois University
R. Duane Skaggs, Morehead State University
Nancy Lynn Tinkham, Rowan University
Jinhui Xu, State University of New York at Buffalo

I want to express my gratitude to the staff at Jones and Bartlett Publishers for their hard work on this text. Thank you to Tim Anderson, Acquisitions Editor; Amy Rose, Production Director; and Melissa Elmore, Editorial Assistant.

Wayne Goddard
Clemson SC

Contents

Regular Languages

This book is about the fundamental capabilities and ultimate limitations of computation. What can be done with what abilities.

We will see three main models of a computer: a finite automaton, a pushdown automaton, and a Turing machine. In parallel with that we will see other formal ways to describe computation and algorithms, through the language of mathematics, including regular expressions and grammars. In the last two parts of the book, we take our computer and ask what can be solved, and if it can be solved, what resources are required, such as speed and memory. Concepts such as finite automata are certainly useful throughout computer science, but even proving something impossible is good because it tells you where not to look, that you have to compromise on some aspect.

The input to our computers is always strings. We discuss this later, but it is true that everything can be converted to questions about strings.

We start with the simplest form of computer, or maybe, machine. For example, an automatic door. It spends all day either open or closed. The design is simple. Open, closed. Or maybe opening, open, closing, closed. Or maybe there's an override. This is the simplest form of a machine: only internal memory, nothing external, just reacting to events. Ladies and gentlemen, I give you the finite automaton.

Any language is necessarily a finite system applied with different degrees of creativity to an infinite variety of situations, . . .   —**David Lodge**

Nature is a self-made machine, more perfectly automated than any automated machine.   —**Eric Hoffer**

Mathematics, rightly viewed, possesses not only truth, but supreme beauty—a beauty cold and austere, like that of sculpture, without appeal to any part of our weaker nature, without the gorgeous trappings of painting or music, yet sublimely pure, and capable of a stern perfection such as only the greatest art can show.   —**Bertrand Russell**

—**Benjamin Disraeli**

I hate definitions.

1

Finite Automata

The most basic model of a computer is the finite automaton. This is a computer without memory; or rather, the amount of memory is fixed, regardless of the size of the input.

1.1 A Finite Automaton Has States

A **string** is a sequence of characters or **symbols**. A finite-state machine or **finite automaton** (FA) is a device that recognizes a collection of strings. (The plural of automaton is automata.) An FA has three components:

1. An **input tape**, which contains a single string
2. A sensor or **head**, which reads the input string one symbol at a time
3. **Memory**, which can be in any one of a finite number of states—so we speak of the **current state** of the automaton

The "program" of the FA prescribes how the symbols that are read affect the current state. The **final state** for a string is the state the automaton is in when it finishes reading the input.

Operating an FA	1. Set the machine to the start state.
	2. If end-of-string then halt.
	3. Read a symbol.
	4. Update the state according to current state and symbol read.
	5. Goto step 2.

An FA can be described by a diagram. In the diagram, each state is drawn as a circle; we sometimes name a state by putting its name inside the circle. Each state has, for each symbol, an arrow showing the next state. The initial or **start state** is shown by an arrow into it from no state.

The purpose of an FA is as a **recognizer**—essentially, it acts like a boolean function. For any FA, certain states are designated as **accept** states and the remainder are **reject** states. An **accept state** is indicated by a double circle in the diagram.

Definition   An FA **accepts** the input string if the final state is an accept state, otherwise it rejects the input string.

Example 1.1   The following is an FA with 3 states called A, B, and C. The start state is A, and C is the only accept state.

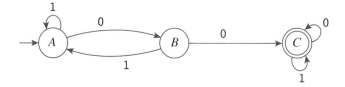

Consider its behavior when the input string is 101001:

Current State	Symbol Read	New State
A	1	A
A	0	B
B	1	A
A	0	B
B	0	C
C	1	C

Here, the final state is C. Similarly, the final state for 11101 is A, and for 0001 it is C.

What does it take to get to the accept state? This machine accepts all strings of 0's and 1's with two consecutive zeroes somewhere.

Example 1.2 Consider the following FA.

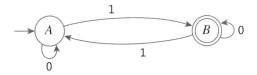

This FA accepts strings like 100 and 0101001 and 11111, and rejects strings like 000 and 0110.

Can you describe exactly which strings this FA accepts?

If you can't wait, then read on. This FA ignores the symbol 0 (it doesn't change state). It only worries about the symbol 1; here it alternates states. The first 1 takes it to state B, the second 1 takes it to state A, the third to state B, and so on. So it is in state B whenever an odd number of 1's have been read.

That is, this machine accepts all strings of 0's and 1's with an odd number of 1's.

In these examples, we simply use letters for the names of states. Sometimes you can find more descriptive names.

1.2 Building FAs

There is no magic method for building FAs. It takes practice and thinking (though some of the machinery in subsequent chapters will be helpful). In this section, we consider how to build an FA for a specific purpose.

First, we need a few more definitions. An **alphabet** is a set of symbols. A **language** is a set of strings, where the strings have symbols from a specific alphabet. The language of an FA is the set of strings it accepts. For example, the language of the first FA from Example 1.1 is the set of all strings with alphabet $\{0, 1\}$ that contain the substring 00.

We often use Σ to denote the alphabet. Often the alphabet will be $\{a, b\}$ or $\{0, 1\}$; though this is abusing the term, we refer to strings from the alphabet $\{0, 1\}$ as **binary** strings. A **unary language** is one where the alphabet has only one symbol.

The **length** of a string is the number of symbols in it. The **empty string** has length 0: it is a string without any symbols and is denoted ε.

Sometimes the obvious natural idea works.

Example 1.3

All binary strings starting with 00.

The approach is to read the first two symbols, and that gives one the answer. The rest of the string is ignored (which corresponds to the automaton never changing state).

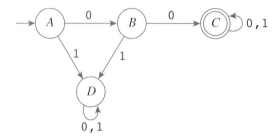

To save clutter on the diagram, you can label an arrow with multiple symbols separated by commas.

If you are interested in the final two symbols, then you have to work a little harder, as we see next.

Example 1.4

All binary strings ending in 00.

Well, the first thing you might do is to think about what happens if the first two symbols are 0. That must take you to an accept state. So, there are at least three states: A, B, and C, where A is the start state, C is an accept state, and a 0 takes you from A to B, and from B to C.

But what happens if you read a 1? Well, if you think about it, this should take the FA back to the start state, no matter what state it is in. Another question is, what happens if you get a 0 in state C? Well, staying in C seems reasonable. This yields the following FA:

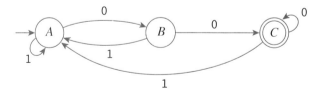

Does this really work? Yes. Perhaps it helps to think about what exactly it means to be in each state. State C means that the previous two symbols were 00, state A means that the previous symbol was 1, and state B means that the last two symbols were 10.

A common type of state is a **trap**. This is a state that, once entered, you can never leave. For example, state C of Example 1.1 is a trap. How can you recognize a trap from the picture? *A trap has no arrow out.* Traps can be used in two ways:

a) As a reject state for partly read strings that will never be accepted
b) As an accept state for partly read strings that will definitely be accepted

Example 1.5   **An FA that accepts all binary strings where 0's and 1's alternate.**

The main idea is a pair of states that oscillate: 0 takes you to one and 1 takes you back again. We also need a trap if ever two consecutive symbols are the same.

One approach is to have a start state that splits into two sub-machines. This gives the following solution:

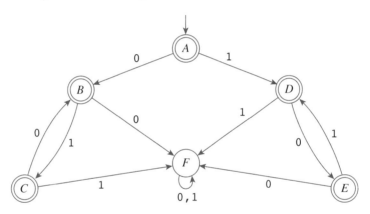

But actually, you can do it with fewer states:

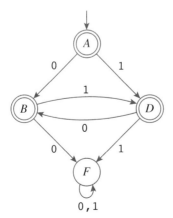

So, although a given FA corresponds to only one language, a given language can have many FAs that accept it.

Note that you must always be careful about the *empty string*: should the FA accept ε or not. (Though, to be fair, this is not always clear from the English description.) In the preceding example, the empty string is accepted because the start state is also an accept state.

Another useful technique is **remembering specific symbols**. In the next example, you must forever remember the first symbol; so the FA splits into two pieces after the first symbol.

Example 1.6 **An FA that accepts all binary strings that begin and end with the same symbol.**

It is clear that the automaton must be in two different states based on the first symbol that is read. After that, you need to keep track of the current symbol just read, in case it turns out to be the final symbol. But that is enough.

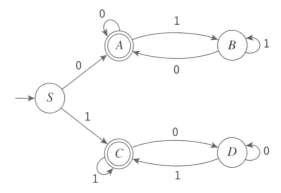

Note that there must not be any connection between the top and bottom halves, since otherwise the FA might forget the first symbol read.

And now:

 For You to Do!

Give an FA for each of the following three languages:

1. All binary strings with at least one 0
2. All binary strings with at most one 0
3. All binary strings starting and ending with 0 (and the string with a single 0 counts)

The solutions to the practice problems are given at the end of the chapter.

1.3 Representing FAs

A diagram is not the only way to represent an FA. Indeed, to feed an FA into a computer you must have another way to represent it. One way to go is called a **transition table**: this is a matrix that lists the new state given the current state and the symbol read.

Example 1.6 (continued)

Here is the transition table for the FA that accepts all binary strings that begin and end with the same symbol.

		Input	
		0	1
State	S	A	C
	A	A	B
	B	A	B
	C	D	C
	D	D	C

We shall see soon a more general type of FA; the FA we have seen so far is actually a deterministic one (sometimes abbreviated DFA). One can provide a **formal definition** of a DFA using the language of mathematics. We may define a deterministic finite automaton as a 5-tuple $(Q, \Sigma, q_0, T, \delta)$ where:

- ■ Q is a finite set of states
- ■ Σ is an alphabet of input symbols
- ■ q_0 is the start state
- ■ T is a subset of Q giving the accept states
- ■ δ is the **transition function** that maps a state and symbol to a state. (In mathematical notation, we say that $\delta \colon Q \times \Sigma \mapsto Q$.) For example, $\delta(r, 1) = s$ means that in state r on reading symbol 1 change to state s.

This approach makes precise what we need to specify for an FA. It also allows us to use mathematical notation to describe one.

Example 1.6 (continued)

And for the previous example, the 5-tuple is $(Q, \Sigma, q_0, T, \delta)$ where

$$Q = \{S, A, B, C, D\}$$
$$\Sigma = \{0, 1\}$$

$$q_0 = S$$
$$T = \{A, C\}$$

δ is given by the previous transition table

EXERCISES

1.1 Give an FA that accepts only the string 0110.

1.2 Give an FA that accepts only binary strings of length 3.

1.3 If in Example 1.1 we make both states B and C accept states, describe in English the strings the FA accepts.

★ **1.4** For the following two FAs, determine which of the strings 0110, 1, 1011010, and 00000 are accepted.

a)

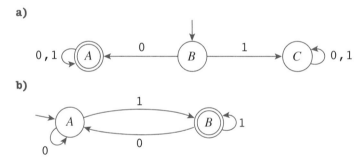

b)

1.5 For the preceding two FAs, describe in English the strings each accepts.

1.6 Draw an FA that accepts any string of 0's and 1's.

1.7 For the following FA, determine which of the strings 0110, 1, 1011010, and 00000 are accepted.

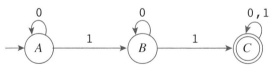

★ **1.8** For the preceding FA, describe in English the strings it accepts.

1.9 Give an FA for each of the following languages:

    a) All binary strings with at least three 1's
    b) All binary strings with an odd number of 1's
    c) All binary strings without 111 as a substring
    d) All binary strings where every *odd* position is a 1

1.10 We can use a spreadsheet program to simulate an FA. This involves storing the FA's transition table as a lookup table. Describe how to simulate an FA using a spreadsheet program.

1.11 Construct an FA that accepts all binary strings with precisely three 1's.

★ **1.12** Construct an FA that accepts all strings of {a, b, c} that contain an odd number of a's.

1.13 Give an FA for the language of all binary strings that have at least three symbols and whose first and last symbols are different.

1.14 Give an FA whose language is the set of strings of a's, b's, and c's that contain abc as a substring.

1.15 Construct an FA that accepts all strings of {a, b} that contain either ab or bba (or both) as substrings.

★ **1.16** Construct an FA that accepts all strings of {a, b, c} whose symbols are in alphabetical order. (For example, aaabcc and ac are okay; abca and cb are not.)

H **1.17** Construct an FA that accepts all binary strings with an even number of 0's and the number of 1's is a multiple of 3.

1.18 Explain in English what the following FA accepts:

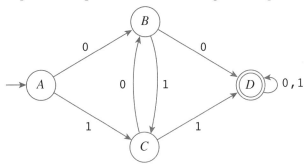

1.19 Explain in English what the following FA accepts:

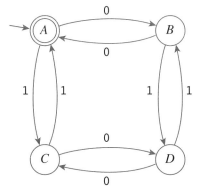

"For You to Do" Exercise Solutions

1.

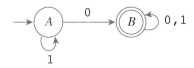

2.

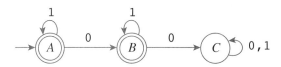

3.

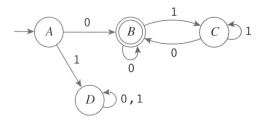

2

Regular Expressions

Often you are faced with the task of recognizing strings of a certain type. For example, suppose you want a method or procedure that recognizes decimal numbers. To write such a method, we need to be clear about what we mean by a decimal number. We can define a decimal number as follows: "Some digits followed maybe by a point and some more digits."

That definition is far too sloppy to be of use. The following is better: "optional minus sign, any sequence of digits, followed by optional point, and if so then optional sequence of digits." To be more precise, we can write the description of a decimal number as a regular expression:

$$(-+\varepsilon)\,\mathrm{D}\,\mathrm{D}^{*}\,(\varepsilon + .\,\mathrm{D}^{*})$$

where D stands for a digit. But then you need to understand what a regular expression is . . . .

2.1 Regular Expressions

A **regular expression** (RE) corresponds to a set of strings; that is, a regular expression describes a language. It is built up using the three regular operations called **union**, **concatenation**, and **star**, described in the following paragraphs. A regular expression uses normal symbols as well as four special symbols:

$$+ \quad {}^{*} \quad (\quad)$$

A regular expression is interpreted using the following rules:

- ■ The parentheses (and) are used for grouping, just as in normal math.
- ■ The plus sign (+) means **union**. Thus, writing

    0 + 1

    means either a zero or a one. We also refer to the + as **or**.
- ■ The **concatenation** of two expressions is obtained by simply writing one after the other without spacing between them. For example,

    (0 + 1) 0

    corresponds to the pair of strings 00 and 10.
- ■ The symbol ε stands for the empty string. Thus, the regular expression

    (0 + 1) (0 + ε)

    corresponds to the four strings 00, 0, 10, 1.
- ■ The asterisk ($*$) is pronounced *star* and means zero or more copies.

    For example, the regular expression

    a*

    corresponds to any string of a's: $\{\varepsilon, a, aa, aaa, \ldots\}$. Also,

    (0 + 1)*

    corresponds to all binary strings. (It's $\varepsilon + (0 + 1) + (0 + 1)(0 + 1) + \ldots$)

Example 2.1   The regular expression

(01)*

corresponds to the set containing ε, 01, 0101, 010101, and so forth.

Example 2.2   What about a regular expression for the language of all binary strings of length at least 2 that begin and end in the same symbol?
    This is given by:

0(0 + 1)*0 + 1(0 + 1)*1

Note too the **precedence** of the regular operators: star first, then concatenation, then or. That is, the *star* always refers to the smallest piece it can, the *or* to the largest.

Example 2.3

Consider the regular expression

$$((0+1)^*1+\varepsilon)\,(00)^*\,00$$

The language of this RE is the collection of all binary strings that end with an even nonzero number of 0's.

There are snares waiting for the unwary. For example, someone proposed the RE

$$(0+1)^*\,(00)^*\,00$$

for this language. But this RE corresponds to any binary string that ends with 00: take any string you like from the $(0+1)^*$ part, take nothing from the $(00)^*$ part, and 00 from the last part.

In general, if you form an RE by the **or** of two REs, call them R and S, then the resulting language is the union of the languages of R and S. This is why $+$ is called the union operation.

If you form an RE by the **concatenation** of two REs, call them R and S, then the resulting language consists of all strings that can be formed by taking one string from the language of R and one string from the language of S and concatenating them.

If you form an RE by taking the star of an RE R, then the resulting language consists of all strings that can be formed by taking any number of strings from the language of R (they need not be the same and they need not be different), and concatenating them.

Indeed, we can talk about the union, concatenation, or star of languages. For example, here is a recursive definition of the star of a language:

Recursive definition of L^*

1. $\varepsilon \in L^*$.
2. If $x \in L^*$ and $y \in L$ then $xy \in L^*$.

Example 2.4

If language L is $\{\mathrm{ma, pa}\}$ and language M is $\{\mathrm{be, bop}\}$, then

$L+M$ is $\{\mathrm{ma, pa, be, bop}\}$.
LM is $\{\mathrm{mabe, mabop, pabe, pabop}\}$.
L^* is $\{\varepsilon, \mathrm{ma, pa, mama}, \ldots, \mathrm{pamamapa}, \ldots\}$.

We also use the following notation.

Notation	If Σ is some alphabet, then Σ^* is the set of all strings using that alphabet.

2.2 Kleene's Theorem

It is not hard to write a recognizer to accept a string if and only if the string is of the required form described by the preceding example regular expressions. But what about a complicated regular expression? Fortunately, there is an algorithm (and hence a program) for doing this. In fact, you can always build a finite automaton.

Example 2.5	Give an FA for the language of the RE

$$(0+1)^*00(0+1)^*$$

This was given in Example 1.1.

In the next chapter we will prove the following:

Kleene's Theorem	There is an FA for a language if and only if there is an RE for the language.

This theorem is not just of theoretical benefit: for, it is often easy to describe a recognition problem by an RE, and it is easy to write a procedure that simulates an FA. The theorem, translated into an algorithm, gives one the bridge to convert an RE into an FA. We will use the term regular language for a language that is accepted by some FA or described by an RE.

2.3 Applications of REs

We mention here a few of the applications of finite automata and regular expressions. Several more are discussed in Chapter 5.

Regular expressions are used in the design of compilers to describe some of the pieces of the language. For example, in Pascal or Java an integer has a certain form, a real number has a certain form, and so forth. The RE for each piece can be automatically converted into an FA that recognizes them. A scanner or **tokenizer** is a program that scans the input and determines and identifies the next piece. A tokenizer is provided as a standard part of Java and Unix.

Regular expressions can also be used for searching a file. For example, suppose in a long document you've written hexadecimal numbers with an h behind, such as 273h or 22h, and your boss now says that hexadecimal numbers should be written with a # in front, such as #273 or #22. Well, if you have a good search-and-replace option (such as in Perl), you can type something like

> find: ([0123456789]+)h
> replace with: #\1

In the find text, the symbol + is like * and stands for one or more copies; the square brackets specify a set of symbols; and the parentheses specify an expression. The \1 in the replacement text means the first expression in the find text.

For You to Do!

Give an RE for each of the following three languages:

1. All binary strings with at least one 0
2. All binary strings with at most one 0
3. All binary strings starting and ending with 0

EXERCISES

2.1 For each RE, state which of the following strings is in the language of the RE: ε, abba, bababb, and baaaa.

   a) $(a+b)^*ab(a+b)^*$
   b) $b^*ab^*ab^*$
   c) $a+(a^*b)^*$

2.2 For each RE, give two strings that are in the corresponding language and two strings that are not:

   a) $a(a+b)^*b$
   b) $a^*a+\varepsilon+b^*$
   c) $(ab+ba)^*$

2.3 Give REs for:

   a) All binary strings with exactly two 1's

   b) All binary strings with a double symbol (contains 00 or 11) somewhere

   c) All binary strings that contain both 00 and 11 as substrings

   d) All binary strings without a double symbol anywhere

★ **2.4** Give an FA for decimal numbers as described at the start of this chapter.

2.5 Give an RE for the language of all binary strings of length at least two that begin and end with the same symbol.

2.6 Give REs and FAs with alphabet $\{a, b\}$ for

   a) All strings containing the substring aaa

   b) All strings not containing the substring aaa

   c) All strings that do not end with aaa

   d) All strings with exactly 3 a's.

   e) All strings with the number of a's divisible by 3.

2.7 Give an RE for the language of Exercise 1.12.

★ **2.8** Give an RE for the language of Exercise 1.13.

2.9 Give an RE for the language of Exercise 1.14.

2.10 Give an RE for the language of Exercise 1.15.

2.11 Give an RE for the language of Exercise 1.16.

★ **2.12** Give an RE for the language of Exercise 1.19.

2.13 Give a regular expression for the complement of the RE 111 with respect to the alphabet $\{0, 1\}$. That is, the RE should allow every possible binary string except for the string 111.

2.14 Does every regular language correspond to only *one* RE? Does every RE correspond to only *one* regular language? Discuss.

2.15 Show that the language of RE $(0^*1^*)^*$ is all binary strings.

★ **2.16** Simplify the following REs (that is, find a simpler RE for the same language):

   a) $(r + \varepsilon)^*$

   b) $ss^* + \varepsilon$

   c) $(\varepsilon + r)(r + s)^*(\varepsilon + r)$

   d) $(r + s + rs + sr)^*$

2.17 In a string, a **block** is a substring in which all symbols are the same and which cannot be enlarged. For example, 0001100 has *three* blocks. Let L be the language consisting of all binary strings such that every block has length 2 or 3. Give both an FA and an RE for L.

Ⓗ **2.18** Let C_n denote the set of all binary numbers that are a multiple of n. Show that C_7 is regular. (Hint: Find an FA.)

2.19 Propose a formal definition of a regular expression in the spirit of the one given for an FA on Page 9.

"For You to Do" Exercise Solutions

1. $(0+1)^*0(0+1)^*$
2. $1^*+1^*01^*$
3. $0(0+1)^*0+0$

In each case several answers are possible.

chapter

3

Nondeterminism

The FAs we defined—and our real-world computers—are deterministic: the program completely specifies a unique action at each stage. But what happens if we allow the machine some flexibility or nondeterminism? And this is not just a theoretical musing: the conversion from RE to FA cannot be performed without introducing nondeterminism.

3.1 Nondeterministic Finite Automata

We define a **nondeterministic** finite automaton as follows. In this automaton, for each state there can be zero, one, two, or more transitions corresponding to a particular symbol of the alphabet. If the automaton gets to a state where there is more than one possible transition corresponding to the input symbol, we say that the automaton **branches**. If the automaton gets to a state where there is no such transition, then that branch of the automaton halts and rejects: we say that it **dies**. Thus, it is possible that some branch accepts and some branch rejects. How do you know whether the string is in the language or not? We say the following.

Definition   A nondeterministic FA (NFA) **accepts** the input string if **there exists** some choice of transitions that leads to an accept state.

Note that this definition is *not* symmetric: one accepting branch is enough for the overall automaton to accept, but every branch must reject for the overall automaton to reject. Also, this is only a model of a computer: nondeterministic machines do not actually exist (though some would disagree).

| Example 3.1 | What does this NFA accept? |

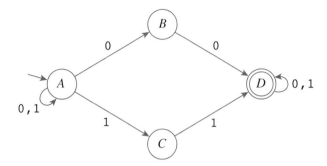

For example, 0110 is accepted because the automaton can proceed $A\,A\,C\,D\,D$. But 101010 is not accepted; any branch that goes to states B or C dies.

In fact, this NFA accepts any binary string that contains 00 or 11 as a substring.

We write **DFA** when we want to specify a deterministic finite automaton, the one defined earlier. If the type doesn't matter, we just write **FA** again.

| Example 3.2 | An easy nondeterministic automaton to build is one for the language of all strings with a particular ending. Here is an NFA that accepts all binary strings that end with 101. To accept strings in the language, the machine stays in state A until it nondeterministically guesses to move to state B at the correct 1. |

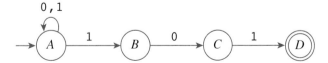

In the following example, we use nondeterminism to look for two patterns "simultaneously."

| Example 3.3 | **An NFA for** $a^* + (ab)^*$ |

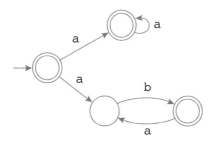

3.2   What Is Nondeterminism?

There are many ways to view nondeterminism. You can think of the machine as guessing the next move: the **"guess and verify"** idea. In this, you assume that the machine is clairvoyant and always guesses correctly the next state to go to. However, the rules are that the machine may make as many guesses as it likes, but it must "check" them. In Example 3.1, the automaton guesses whether the start of the double symbol has been reached or not; it checks its guess by reading the next two symbols. If the string is not in the language, then no sequence of guesses can lead to acceptance.

Alternatively, you can think of nondeterminism as a **computation tree** growing downward. At each node the children are all the possible successors. You may then talk about a branch of the computational tree: the string is accepted exactly when one of the branches ends in an accept state.

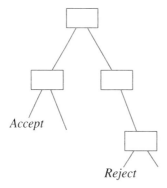

This implies that you can (in some sense) simulate an NFA using guess and backtracking—more on this later.

3.3 ε-Transitions

We also allow ε-transitions: arrows labeled with the empty string. These allow the machine to change state without consuming an input symbol. For example, if the overall language is the union of two languages, such a transition allows the machine to guess which part the input string is in.

Example 3.4 What about an NFA that accepts all binary strings where the last symbol is 0 or which contain only 1's?

Here is one:

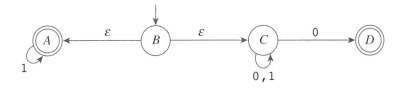

Example 3.5 Here is another NFA for a* + (ab)*, which was originally considered in Example 3.3:

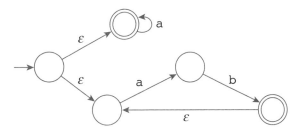

We can provide a similar **formal definition** for an NFA. It is a 5-tuple $(Q, \Sigma, q_0, T, \delta)$ where as before:

- Q is a finite set of states.
- Σ is an alphabet of input symbols.
- q_0 is the start state.
- T is a subset of Q giving the accept states.
- δ is the transition function.

The difference is that now the transition function specifies a *set* of states rather than a state: it maps $Q \times (\Sigma \cup \{\varepsilon\})$ to { subsets of Q }. For example, in the NFA of Example 3.4, you have $\delta(A, 1) = \{A\}$, $\delta(B, \varepsilon) = \{A, C\}$, and $\delta(D, 0) = \emptyset$.

 For You to Do!

1. Give an NFA for the set of all binary strings that have either the number of 0's odd, or the number of 1's not a multiple of 3, or both.

3.4   Kleene's Theorem Revisited

Surprisingly perhaps, nondeterminism does not add to the power of a finite automaton.

Kleene's Theorem

The following are equivalent for a language L:

1. There is a DFA for L.
2. There is an NFA for L.
3. There is an RE for L.

This theorem is proved in three steps. In fact, we produce an algorithm that does the conversion:

$$(3) \Longrightarrow (2) \Longrightarrow (1) \Longrightarrow (3).$$

Thus, if you know that a language is regular, then you know that it is accepted by some DFA, by some NFA, and described by some RE.

3.5   Conversion from RE to NFA

We consider here the conversion from RE to NFA. This is a recursive construction.

Because an RE is built up recursively, we need to (1) describe an NFA for each symbol and for ε; and (2) show that if there exists NFAs for REs A and B, then there exist NFAs for $A + B$, AB, and A^*. (Why will this constitute a proof?)

Converting from RE to NFA (Outline)

0. If the RE is the empty string, then output simple NFA.
1. Else if the RE is a single symbol, then output simple NFA.
2. Else if RE has form $A + B$, then combine the NFAs for A and B.
3. Else if RE has form AB, then combine the NFAs for A and B.
4. Else if RE has form A^*, then extend the NFA for A.

What remains is to work out how to combine or extend these NFAs.

1) An NFA for a single symbol C consists of two states q_0 and q_1. The first is the start state and the second the accept state. There is one transition from q_0 to q_1 labeled with that symbol:

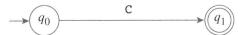

2) Armed with an NFA M_A for A and M_B for B, here is one for $A + B$. Add a new start state with ε-transitions to the original start states of both M_A and M_B. The machine guesses which of A or B the input is in.

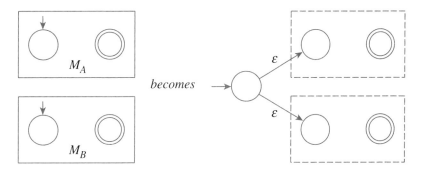

3) Here is one for the concatenation AB. Start with NFAs M_A and M_B. The first step is to put ε-transitions from the accept states of M_A to the start state of M_B. Then, you must make the original accept states of M_A reject.

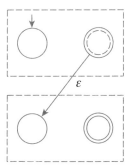

4) Here is one for A^*. The idea is to allow the machine to cycle from the accept state back to the start state. The natural try is to make the start state accepting and put ε-transitions from the accept states back to the start state. But this doesn't quite work. Why? Well, that might add

strings to the language (that previously ended in the start state which wasn't accepting).

What you can do is build a new start state, which is the only accept state; then put an ε-transition from it to the old start state and from the old accept states to it; and change every old accept state to a reject state.

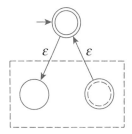

Example 3.6   Consider applying the preceding algorithm to build an NFA for $0 + 10^*$. Start by building NFAs for the 0, the 1, and the 0^*, then combine the latter two, and finally merge the pieces.

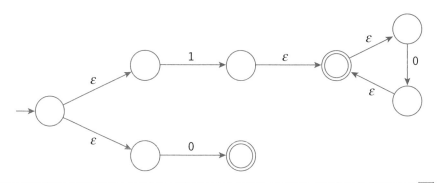

Usually the resulting NFA can be easily simplified, as it can in this case.

3.6 Conversion from NFA to DFA

We show next how to convert from an NFA to a DFA. This algorithm is called the **subset construction**. For this, we need to re-examine the workings of an NFA.

Think of how you would determine whether an NFA accepts a given string. The simplest idea is to try systematically all possible transitions. This certainly works, but is not very efficient and takes time exponential in the length of the input.

A better idea is to at each step keep track of the set of states the NFA could be in. The key point is that you can determine the set at one step if you know (only) the set at the previous step.

Example 3.7

Consider the behavior of the NFA from Example 3.1 on the string 10100. At the start it is in state A. After reading the 1, the machine is in state A or state C. What happens when the 0 is read? If the machine is in state A, it can choose to go to state A or B. If the machine is in state C it dies. So after the second symbol, the set of states the machine can be in is $\{A, B\}$. Then, when it reads the third symbol, if in state A it goes to $\{A, C\}$, but if in B it dies.

Thus, if we are simulating the machine, it is sufficient to keep track of the set of states the machine could be in. The machine would proceed:

$$\{A\} \xrightarrow{1} \{A, C\} \xrightarrow{0} \{A, B\} \xrightarrow{1} \{A, C\} \xrightarrow{0} \{A, B\} \xrightarrow{0} \{A, B, D\}$$

Does the machine accept 10100? Yes: it can be in an accept state (D) after reading the final symbol.

But there is only a finite number of sets of states. So, the conversion process is to start with the start state, and then to use a systematic process (for example, a breadth-first search) to discover the rest of the diagram. Note that some sets of states might never occur.

Conversion from NFA (without ε-transitions) to DFA

0. Each state is given by a set of states from the original.
1. Start state is labeled $\{q_0\}$ where q_0 was original start state.
2. While (some state of DFA is missing a transition) do:
   compute the transition by combining the possibilities for each symbol in the set.
3. Make into accept state any set that contains at least one original accept state.

Example 3.8

The following DFA is the result of applying the preceding algorithm to the NFA from Example 3.1.

For example, consider the state $\{A, B, D\}$. On a 1, the NFA, if in state A, can go to states A or C, if in state B dies, and if in state D stays in state D. Thus, on a 1 the DFA goes from $\{A, B, D\}$ to $\{A, C, D\}$. Both of these are accept states because they contain D.

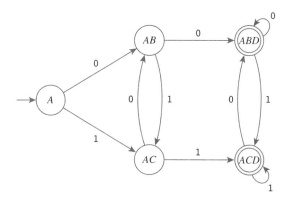

Note that the subset construction does not necessarily give the smallest DFA that does the job. For example, a DFA with fewer states than the one in the previous example was given in Exercise 1.18.

If there are ε-transitions, then you have to adjust the process slightly. Do the following.

Conversion from NFA (with ε-transitions) to DFA	As before, except: **1.** The start state becomes the old start state and every state reachable from there by ε-transitions. **2.** When one calculates the states reachable from a state, one includes all states reachable by ε-transitions **after** the destination state.

Example 3.9

This is the result of applying the preceding algorithm to the NFA from Example 3.4.

The start state consists of A and the two states you can reach by ε-transitions; the start state is thus $\{A, B, C\}$.

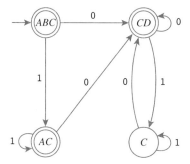

3.7   Conversion from FA to RE

Finally, we show how to convert from an FA to an RE. One way to do this is to generalize even further the notion of an FA. In a **generalized FA** (GFA), each transition is given by an RE. We restrict our attention to the following case:

> *There is a unique accept state, there is no transition out of the accept state, and no transition into the start state (not even a loop).*

Using ε-transitions, you may easily convert any NFA into this form. (How? Left as an exercise.)

What you do now is to build a series of GFAs. At each step, one state other than the start or accept state is removed; the removed state (and its transitions) is replaced by transitions that have the same effect. In particular, if there is a transition a from state 1 to state 2, a transition b from state 2 to state 2, and a transition c from state 2 to state 3, you can achieve the same effect by a transition ab*c from state 1 to state 3.

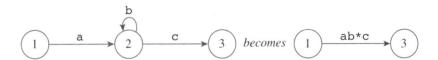

Of course, you need to be convinced that the language accepted by the machine doesn't change. Note, too, that two transitions joining the same pair of states can be merged using the OR of the REs.

Repeat this process until only two states remain; the start and accept states. The label on the single transition joining the two states is a regular expression that corresponds to the original NFA. This process can be summarized as follows:

Conversion from FA to RE

0. Convert to FA of the right form (no arc into start, no arc out of unique accept).

1. While (more than two states) do
    remove a state and replace by appropriate transitions.

2. Read RE off the remaining transition.

Example 3.10 Here is the NFA of Example 3.3 adjusted to have a unique accept state.

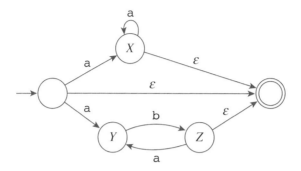

If we eliminate state X, we get

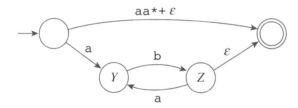

If we eliminate state Z, we get

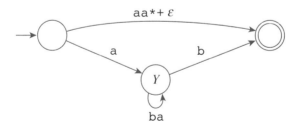

If we eliminate state Y, we get

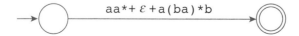

For You to Do!

2. Convert the NFA from Example 3.2 to a DFA using the subset construction.

3. Convert the DFA from Example 3.9 to an RE using the preceding method.

EXERCISES

3.1 Give an NFA for the language of the RE $a^*b + b^*a$.

3.2 Give an NFA for the set of all binary strings that have 0 as the second-to-last symbol.

3.3 Give an FA for the set of strings with alphabet $\{a, b\}$ that contain both or neither aa and bb as substrings.

★ **3.4** Give an FA for the set of strings with alphabet $\{a, b, c\}$ that have a substring of length 3 containing each of the symbols.

3.5 Show that every finite language has an FA.

3.6 Show how to modify an NFA to have a unique accept state with no transition ending at the start state and no transition starting at the accept state.

3.7 If M is a DFA accepting language B, then exchanging the accept and reject states gives a new DFA accepting the complement of B. Does this work for an NFA? Discuss.

★ **3.8** For the following NFA, use the subset construction to produce an equivalent DFA.

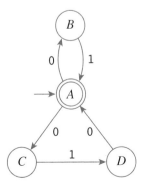

3.9 For the following NFA, use the subset construction to produce an equivalent DFA.

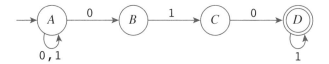

3.10 Consider the RE $(0 + 01^*)^*$.

    a) By following (the spirit of) the text algorithm, produce an equivalent NFA.

    b) Describe in English the language of this RE.

3.11 Provide an algorithm to tell if the language is infinite if the input is

    a) an RE

    b) an NFA

★ **3.12** Use the subset construction to convert the following NFA to a DFA.

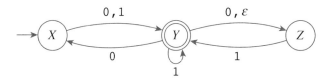

3.13 Use the GFA algorithm to convert the FA of Example 3.9 to an RE.

3.14 Use the GFA algorithm to convert the final FA of Chapter 1 (Exercise 1.19) to an RE.

3.15 Discuss the growth in the conversions. If the original object has size n, how large (very roughly) can the new object be?

    a) Conversion from RE to NFA

    b) Conversion from NFA to DFA

    Ⓗ **c)** Conversion from FA to RE

3.16 (TERM PAPER) "Nondeterminism and randomness. Real or imaginary?"

"For You to Do" Exercise Solutions

1.

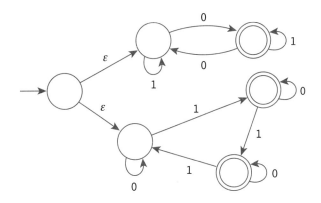

2.

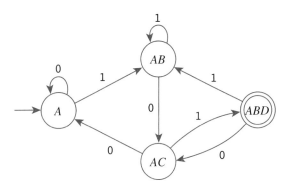

3. $(0 + 11^*0)(0 + 11^*0)^* + \varepsilon + 11^*$

chapter
4

Properties of
Regular Languages

There are severe limits to the type of recognition problems that can be handled with an FA. But to actually prove that a language is not regular requires some ideas; these are formalized in the notions of distinguishable strings and the infamous Pumping Lemma. We start, however, with some closure properties of the set of regular languages.

4.1 Closure Properties

A set is closed under an operation if applying that operation to any members of the set yields a member of the set. For example, the set of integers is closed under multiplication but not under division.

Fact	The set of regular languages is closed under each of the Kleene operations (union, concatenation, and star).

What does this mean? Assume that L_1 and L_2 are regular languages. Then the result says that each of $L_1 \cup L_2$, $L_1 L_2$, and L_1^* is a regular language.

Proof	The easiest way to proceed is to show that the REs for L_1 and L_2 can be combined or adjusted to form the RE for the combination language. For example, the RE for $L_1 L_2$ is obtained by simply writing down the RE for L_1 followed by the RE for L_2. The remaining cases are left as an exercise.

♦

It is important to remember that this question is a property about sets of languages, not about individual strings.

Fact   The set of regular languages is (a) closed under complementation, and (b) closed under intersection.

Proof (a) The statement says that if L is a regular language, then so is its complement. The complement of a language, written $\overline{L}$, is its complement as a set: all those strings not in L but with the same alphabet.

To see this fact, look at the deterministic FA for L. To get an FA for $\overline{L}$, simply interchange the accept and reject states. (As an exercise in the previous chapter noted, this interchange does not work with a nondeterministic machine.)

(b) This statement says that if L_1 and L_2 are regular languages, then so is their intersection $L_1 \cap L_2$. To see this, you can use the first part. Then, there is the Venn diagram relation (called de Morgan's law):

$$L_1 \cap L_2 = \overline{(\overline{L_1} \cup \overline{L_2})}$$

This gives you a procedure to produce an FA for $L_1 \cap L_2$.   ♦

The proof of Part (b) actually gives an algorithm (sort of) for producing a DFA for $L_1 \cap L_2$ given the DFAs for L_1 and L_2. Namely, take the DFA for L_1 and DFA for L_2. Interchange accept and reject to yield DFAs for $\overline{L_1}$ and $\overline{L_2}$. Union them (add new start with ε-transitions). Do the subset construction to convert to a deterministic machine. Then interchange accept and reject. Whew!

But there is another algorithm for constructing the intersection called the **product** construction. The idea comes from what you would like to do: you would like to run the string simultaneously through both machines. The solution is to keep track of the **pair** of states from each machine.

In particular, the product automaton has one state for every pair of states from the original machines. The start state is the pair of start states, and the accept states are those where *both* states are accept states.

For example, suppose L_1 is the set of strings with an even number of 0's, and L_2 is the set of strings with an even number of 1's. Then the FAs for these languages both have two states:

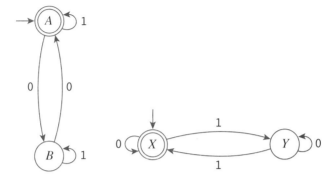

And so the FA for the intersection $L_1 \cap L_2$ has four states:

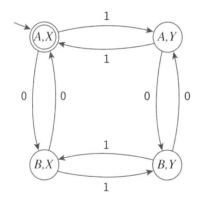

The formal definition of an FA can make this construction look succinct. The **Cartesian product** of two sets A and B, denoted by $A \times B$, is the set $\{(a, b) : a \in A, b \in B\}$. Say L_1 is accepted by automaton M_1 with 5-tuple $(Q_1, \Sigma, q_1, T_1, \delta_1)$ and L_2 is accepted by automaton M_2 with 5-tuple $(Q_2, \Sigma, q_2, T_2, \delta_2)$. Then $L_1 \cap L_2$ is accepted by the automaton $(Q_1 \times Q_2, \Sigma, (q_1, q_2), T_1 \times T_2, \delta)$ where $\delta((r, s), x) = (\delta_1(r, x), \delta_2(s, x))$.

4.2 Distinguishable Strings

Of course, questions about closure would be meaningless without languages that are not regular, which we call the **nonregular** languages.

Example 4.2 Consider the string 0^n1^n; this notation means n 0's followed by n 1's. Define the set B by

$$B = \{0^n1^n : n \geq 0\} = \{\varepsilon, 01, 0011, 000111, \dots\}$$

No FA exists for this language.

An argument is the following. Suppose that the input string is valid in the sense that it is a sequence of 0's followed by a series of 1's. The machine has to **count** the number of 0's: that is, at the end of the sequence of 0's it must be in a state unique to the number of 0's that were read. But the machine has only fixed finite memory, while the input string is arbitrarily long, and the number of 0's can be arbitrarily large. So the FA has an impossible job.

That is, B is nonregular.

The point is that an FA has only a fixed amount of memory: the information contained in its state. An FA corresponds to a computer with no external memory, just a fixed set of bits that it can manipulate. Note that you can make the memory as large as you want, but once the FA is built, that is that and the memory cannot be expanded.

To make this more precise and more generally applicable, we need some tools. One idea is the concept of distinguishable strings. We say that two strings x and y are **indistinguishable with respect to** L if for every string z, it holds that $xz \in L$ if and only if $yz \in L$. Otherwise, they are called **distinguishable.** That is, x and y are distinguishable with respect to L if there is some suffix z that can be added such that $xz \in L$ and $yz \notin L$ or vice versa.

Theorem Assume M is an FA accepting language L, and let x and y be distinguishable strings with respect to L. Then M must be in a different state after reading x than after reading y.

Proof Suppose the strings x and y put M in the same state. Then for any string z the strings xz and yz put M in the same state. So, if one of xz and yz accepts and one rejects, we have a problem. The only solution is that x and y must put M in different states: the machine must remember which of x or y it has read.

♦

A set of strings is called **pairwise distinguishable** if every pair of strings in it are distinguishable. By the preceding logic, there must be a different state for each string in the set:

Corollary   If $\mathcal{D}_L$ is a set of pairwise distinguishable strings with respect to L, then any FA for L has at least $|\mathcal{D}_L|$ states. In particular, if $\mathcal{D}_L$ is infinite then L is not regular.

Example 4.2 (continued)   So, back to the language $B = \{0^n 1^n : n \geq 0\}$. We claim that the set $\mathcal{D}_B = \{0^j : j \geq 0\}$ is pairwise distinguishable. Well, take any two strings in $\mathcal{D}_B$; say 0^j and $0^{j'}$ with $j \neq j'$. Then appending 1^j to the first produces a string in B, while appending 1^j to the second produces a string not in B; that is, 0^j and $0^{j'}$ are distinguishable. Because $\mathcal{D}_B$ is infinite, B is not regular.

Example 4.3   Consider the language of Example 4.1. The set $\{\varepsilon, 0, 1, 01\}$ is pairwise distinguishable. So the FA we constructed has the fewest states possible.

We have shown that if there is an infinite set of distinguishable strings for a language, then that language is not regular. There is actually a converse to this; that is, if the language is not regular, then there is guaranteed to be such an infinite set. This result is part of what is called the Myhill–Nerode theorem. In fact, there is a connection between the smallest number of states of an FA and the largest set of pairwise distinguishable strings. Some of the ideas and results are discussed in the exercises.

4.3   The Pumping Lemma

The Pumping Lemma says that every regular language has a certain repetitiveness about it. The lemma can be a bit daunting at first sight.

We will use the following notation. If v is a string, then $|v|$ denotes the length of v. Further, v^3 denotes three consecutive copies of v, and so on.

Pumping Lemma	Let A be a regular language accepted by a DFA with k states. Then, for any string z in A with at least k symbols, you can find an early internal subsegment that can be pumped. That is, z can be split as uvw where:

- v is nonempty
- $|uv| \leq k$
- uv^iw is in A for all $i \geq 0$

Proof

Follow the sequence of states around the DFA on the input z. Let q be the first state that occurs a second time. This repeat must happen by the time k symbols are read (because then the automaton has been in $k+1$ states). Then split the string z as follows:

- String u is the portion up to the first visit to state q.
- String v is the portion between the first and second visit.
- String w is the remainder of the input.

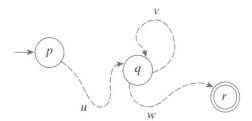

Now the point is that the DFA is in the same state q no matter whether it has read u, uv, uv^2, and so on (it is deterministic). It follows that the DFA is in the same state r no matter whether it has read uw, uvw, or uv^2w. Hence, uv^iw is in A for all $i \geq 0$. ◆

The Pumping Lemma cannot be used to show that a language is regular. Rather, it is used to show that a language is nonregular, by showing that the lemma is contradicted. The art of using the Pumping Lemma is to choose a suitable string z whose pumping causes a contradiction.

Example 4.4 Consider again the language $B = \{\, 0^n1^n : n \geq 0 \,\}$ from Example 4.2.

Suppose B were regular.

Then B would be accepted by a DFA with k states.

Consider the specific string $z = 0^k1^k$. This is in B.

Split $z = uvw$ according to the Pumping Lemma.

Then, because $|uv| \leq k$, it follows that v is composed entirely of 0's.

But then uw is not in B (because it has fewer 0's than 1's).

And this is a contradiction of the Pumping Lemma.

It is important to follow the logic once. But the preceding argument can be used as a template. Note that the user has only to find *one* z that cannot be pumped, but must show that there is a problem with *every* possible split.

Example 4.5 Recall that a **palindrome** is a word that reads the same backward as it does forward (such as "level"). Let P be the set of all palindromes for alphabet $\{a, b\}$. This language is nonregular. Here is the proof using the Pumping Lemma.

Suppose P were regular. Then it would be accepted by a DFA with, say, k states. Consider the string $z = a^kba^k$. Split $z = uvw$ according to the Pumping Lemma. Then, because $|uv| \leq k$, it follows that v is always a string of a's. Thus, none of uw, uv^2w, and so forth is in P. This is a contradiction of the Pumping Lemma, and so our supposition is false.

  For You to Do!   Define E as the language of all binary strings with an equal number of 0's and 1's.

1. Show that E is not regular by finding an infinite set of pairwise distinguishable strings.

2. Show that E is not regular by showing that it contradicts the Pumping Lemma.

4.1 Show that the set of regular languages is closed under reversal. That is, if L is regular, then so is $\{\, x^R : x \in L \,\}$ where x^R denotes the reversal of string x.

4.2 Give an example to show each of the following for languages L_1 and L_2:

    a) If $L_1 \subseteq L_2$ and L_2 is regular, then L_1 can be regular or nonregular.

    b) If L_1 and L_2 are nonregular, then $L_1 \cap L_2$ can be regular or nonregular.

    c) If L_1 and L_2 are nonregular, then $L_1 \cup L_2$ can be regular or nonregular.

4.3 Suppose language L is accepted by FA M. Let L^E be the subset of L consisting of those strings in L of even length. Show how to convert M to an FA for L^E.

★ **4.4** Show that regularity is closed under prefixes. That is, if L is regular, then so is $\{\, x : \text{there is } y \text{ such that } xy \in L \,\}$.

4.5 Let P_m be the set of all binary strings with a 1 in the mth to last symbol (and at least m symbols). For example, P_1 is the set of all strings ending with a 1. Describe an NFA that accepts P_m and uses $m + 1$ states.

4.6 (Continuation of the previous question.)

    a) Explain why it follows that there is a DFA that accepts P_m that has 2^{m+1} states.

    b) Show that there is a DFA that accepts P_m that has 2^m states.

    c) Prove that you need at least 2^m states for a DFA for P_m.

4.7 In a spell checker, it is useful to check whether the given word is one symbol away from a word in the dictionary. For a language L, define L' to the set of all strings obtainable by altering at most one symbol in a string of L. For example, if L is CAT, DOG, then L' is AAT, BAT, CAT, . . . ,ZAT,. . . ,AOG,. . . ,DOZ. Show how to convert an FA for L into one for L'.

★ **4.8** Prove that the set of all strings of a and b with more a's than b's is nonregular.

4.9 Consider the set of all strings with the alphabet $\{\#\}$ with length a perfect square. Show that this language is nonregular.

4.10 Consider the set of all strings with the alphabet $\{\#\}$ with length a prime number. Show that this language is nonregular.

4.11 Show that $\{\, x\#x : x \in \{0,1\}^* \,\}$ is nonregular. (The hash mark/pound sign is a special symbol that should only occur in the middle of the input string.)

★ **4.12** For each of the following languages, state whether it is regular or not. If not, give a proof that it is nonregular.

    a) $\{\, (\text{ab})^n : n > 100 \,\}$

    b) $\{\, (\text{ab})^n : n < 100 \,\}$

    c) The set of binary strings with both the number of 0's and the number of 1's divisible by 100.

4.13 For each of the following languages, state whether it is regular or not. If not, give a proof that it is nonregular.

    a) The set of binary strings with equal number of occurrences of the substrings 01 and 10.

    b) The set of binary nonpalindromes.

    c) $\{a^{2^n} : n \geq 0\}$

4.14 Explain what is wrong with the following "proof" that the language L of the RE a^*b^* is nonregular.

> *Suppose L were regular. Then it would be accepted by a DFA with, say, k states. Consider the string $z = 0^k 1^k$. Split $z = uvw$ with $v = 01$. Then uv^2w is not in L. This is a contradiction of the Pumping Lemma, and so our supposition is false.*

4.15 Consider the language $B = \{0^n 1^n : n \geq 0\}$. Show that a subset of B is regular if and only if it is finite.

★ **4.16** Show that for any fixed m and n, the unary language $\{\#^{m+ni} : i \geq 0\}$ is regular.

4.17 (Continuation of the previous question.) Call a unary language an **arithmetic progression** if it is the set $\{\#^{m+ni} : i \geq 0\}$ for some m and n.

    a) Show that if a unary language is the union of a finite set and a finite number of arithmetic progressions, then it is regular.

    b) Show that if a unary language is regular, then it is the union of a finite set and a finite number of arithmetic progressions.

4.18 Let us use the notation $x \equiv_L y$ to mean that strings x and y are indistinguishable with respect to language L.

    a) Show that $\equiv_L$ is an **equivalence relation**; that is, for all strings x, y, z, the following hold:

        (i) $x \equiv_L x$

        (ii) If $x \equiv_L y$, then $y \equiv_L x$

        (iii) If $x \equiv_L y$ and $y \equiv_L z$, then $x \equiv_L z$.

    b) Show that $\equiv_L$ is a **right congruence**; that is, for all strings x, y, z, the following holds: If $x \equiv_L y$, then $xz \equiv_L yz$.

4.19 (Continuation of previous question.) The equivalence relation $\equiv_L$ partitions the set Σ^* of all possible strings into classes $C_1, C_2, \ldots$ where the strings in each class are pairwise indistinguishable.

    a) Show that if $\equiv_L$ partitions Σ^* into an infinite number of classes, then there is an infinite set of pairwise distinguishable strings for L.

    b) Show that if there is an infinite set of pairwise distinguishable strings for L, then $\equiv_L$ partitions Σ^* into an infinite number of classes.

    c) Show that if $\equiv_L$ partitions Σ^* into a finite number of classes, then there is an FA for L.

d) Show that if there is an FA for L, then $\equiv_L$ partitions Σ^* into a finite number of classes.

4.20 Convince your grandmother that there is no FA that accepts the language of binary strings with an equal number of 0's and 1's.

"For You to Do" Exercise Solutions

1. Let $\mathcal{D}_E$ be the set of all strings containing only 0's. Then for $i \neq j$ the strings 0^i and 0^j are distinguishable with respect to E, since $0^i 1^i \in E$ but $0^j 1^i \notin E$. The set $\mathcal{D}_E$ is infinite, and so E is nonregular.

2. Suppose E were regular. Then it would be accepted by a DFA with, say, k states. Consider the string $z = 0^k 1^k$. Split $z = uvw$ according to the Pumping Lemma. Then since $|uv| \leq k$, it follows that v is always a string of 0's. Thus none of uw, $uv^2 w$, etc. is in E. This is a contradiction of the Pumping Lemma.

5

Applications of Finite Automata

So we have seen some of the theory of finite automata. They and their ideas are surprisingly common in computing. In this brief chapter, we discuss some of the places that they are used.

5.1 String Processing

Consider problems involving strings. A standard task is to find all occurrences of a short string, called the *pattern string*, within a long string, called the *text string*. For example, if the pattern is ana and the text is bananarama's ana, then there are three occurrences of the pattern. Apart from use in editors, this type of question also arises in biology: the text string is the organism's DNA sequence encoded as a string, and the pattern string some DNA sequence of interest.

The naive algorithm considers every possible letter of the text as the starting point of the pattern and takes time proportional to the product of the two lengths. The advantage of this approach is its simplicity.

A simple improvement is to use an FA to process the text; in particular, *the DFA for all strings that end with the specified pattern string*. This choice enables you to examine each symbol of the text only once. This is the basis of the Knuth-Morris-Pratt algorithm; they also showed how to build the DFA quickly. The end result is an algorithm that runs in time proportional to the length of the text.

Example 5.1 Suppose you want to know all occurrences of the pattern 1001 in a text string. The approach is to construct the DFA for all strings ending in 1001.

Then, feed the text string through this one symbol at a time. Every time the accept state q_4 is reached, the current position in the text string is printed out.

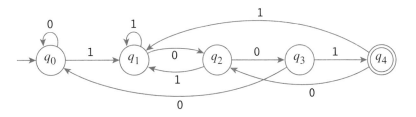

5.2 Finite-State Machines

Finite automata are also used in networks. For example, a communications device is often designed to be in a fixed number of states and to respond to a fixed number of events. For each event, the device's program tells it what action to perform and which state to change to. Here, events such as "receive message" or "timer expires" replace the symbols on the transitions.

The result is usually called a **finite-state machine**: an FA together with actions on the arcs. Here is a trivial example for a communication link:

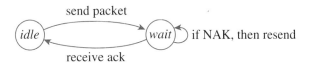 if NAK, then resend

Finite-state machines are also used in specifying the behavior of computer-generated characters, called **bots**, in a game. You get pictures like the following:

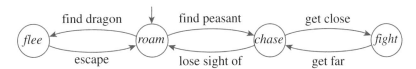

Although the finite-state approach sounds simplistic, and certainly does restrict the range of behaviors of a bot, the advantage is that it's easy to use. Indeed, you can use a metalanguage to specify the diagram and use automated tools to convert to the code.

5.3 Statecharts

Many tasks can be broken up into a set of states and actions to take. For example, the action of dialing on a land-line phone starts with the state of hearing the dial tone. Then the person moves to the state of dialing a number. And so on. **Statecharts** provide a notation for specifying the operation of such processes. These were introduced by Harel in 1987 and are now part of the Unified Modeling Language (UML). Statecharts extend FA diagrams with possibilities such as concurrency, exclusive-or, and hierarchical structures with refinement and superstates.

Example 5.2   Here might be a simplified statechart for a stopwatch.

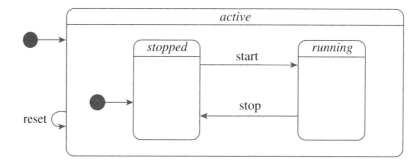

Apart from clarifying the design, the statechart is also useful in code generation in that there are programs that automatically convert the statechart into a program shell.

5.4 Lexical Analysis

The first step in compiling a Java or C program is called **lexical analysis**. This process isolates keywords, identifiers, operators, and so forth, while eliminating symbols such as comments that are irrelevant for future processing. The input to a lexical analyzer is thus the source code as a string, and the output is a sequence of units called tokens.

A **token** is a category, for example, "identifier" or "relation operator." The **lexeme** is the specific instance of the token. Keywords are often separate tokens.

Example 5.3

The code snippet

```
for i = 1 to max do
    x[i] = 0;
```

might have the token sequence

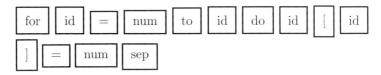

A programming language is not given by a regular expression. But there are portions that are regular expressions (e.g., numeric constants), and these constitute tokens. For example, the reserved word `then` and variable names can be described by the following extended regular expressions:

token	RE
then	then
variable name	[a-zA-Z][a-zA-Z0-9]*

where the RE for the variable name says it is any string of alphanumeric characters that starts with a letter.

The lexical analyzer replaces each token by a single value or lexeme. In principle, it goes through the source string one symbol at a time. But in practice it must read ahead to see where the current token ends. If `then` is read, it's not clear until the next symbol is read if this is a reserved word or an identifier, such as `thence`. So the lexical analyzer must be able to back up if it reads the next symbol and that's a new token. Also, it is implicit in the definition of the next token that it is the *longest* initial segment that fits one of the token definitions.

As each token is identified, there may be appropriate actions to take. For example, when it identifies a number, the lexical analyzer should also calculate the value of the number. One way to do this is to modify the FA to calculate the value as it goes. The lexical analyzer also keeps track of the variables that have been declared through what is called the symbol table. For example, in strongly typed languages such as Java and C, every variable must be declared before use.

There is a utility distributed with Unix called Lex. It is a program that produces C code for a lexical analyzer. The user supplies the definitions of the tokens and the actions that each token should cause. Approaching lexical analysis in this way has its advantages. The input file to Lex is easily modified if changes are to be made. It is also easier to convince yourself of the correctness of the Lex input than if you wrote a lexical analyzer from scratch.

5.1 Draw a DFA for all binary strings ending in 10110.

5.2 Sketch a statechart or a finite-state machine that would represent the operation of a telephone.

5.3 Draw a DFA that accepts all strings that represent decimal numbers (such as 3.1415). Add actions to the transitions so that it calculates the value of the number as it reads the string.

5.4 (TERM PAPER) Take one of the applications mentioned here and investigate further.

SUMMARY

An alphabet is a set of symbols. A string is a finite sequence of symbols drawn from some alphabet. A language is any set of strings. The empty string is denoted ε.

A finite automaton (FA) is a device that recognizes a language. It has finite memory and an input tape; each input symbol that is read causes the machine to update its state based on its current state and the symbol read. The machine accepts the input if it is in an accept state at the end of the string; otherwise, the input is rejected.

A regular expression (RE) is built up from individual symbols using the three Kleene operators: union (+), concatenation, and star (*). The star of a language is obtained by all possible ways of concatenating strings of the language, repeats allowed; the empty string is always in the star of a language.

A nondeterministic finite automaton (NFA) can have zero, one, or multiple transitions corresponding to a particular symbol. It is defined to accept the input if there exists some choice of transitions that cause the machine to end up in an accept state. Nondeterminism can also be viewed as a tree, or as a "guess-and-verify" concept. You can also have ε-transitions, where the NFA can change state without consuming an input symbol.

Kleene's theorem says that the following are equivalent for a language: there is an FA for it; there is an NFA for it; and there is an RE for it. The proof provides an algorithm to convert from one form to another; the conversion from NFA to DFA is the subset construction.

A regular language is one that has an FA or an RE. Regular languages are closed under union, concatenation, star, and complementation. To show that a language is nonregular, you can show that there is an infinite set of pairwise distinguishable strings, or use the Pumping Lemma and show that there is some string that cannot be pumped.

Applications of finite automata include string-matching algorithms, network protocols, and lexical analyzers.

Many of the models in this text can be demonstrated with an interactive visualization and teaching tool for formal languages titled JFLAP. JFLAP is an acronym that stands for Java Formal Language and Automata Package. JFLAP allows users to create and operate on automata, grammars, L-systems, and regular expressions. It is written in Java, hence it runs on most platforms. The software program is available as a free download at www.jflap.org. Please visit the website to register along with the thousands of other students that currently enjoy this interactive tool.

The JFLAP package implements several components. For example, it handles construction of FAs and other models. It also handles the conversion and simulation algorithms discussed in this text, not just the answers. JFLAP will walk the user through each step.

JFLAP allows for and encourages experimentation. One could change one piece and have JFLAP recalculate the result. There are additional models offered with JFLAP. For example, check out JFLAPs L-systems for its vivid pictures.

Context-Free Languages

In the first part of the book, we investigated regular languages. We saw a model computer that recognizes regular languages and a regular expression that generates regular languages. Indeed, several interesting languages are regular. But we saw that some languages that are simple to describe do not fall into this class; you need more power.

So we go in search of a larger family of languages. We now enhance the automaton by giving it some external storage. This storage will initially be in the form of a stack. This is perhaps not the most obvious choice, but it has proved over time to be the most appropriate next level. We shall see that this allows some nonregular languages to be recognized, but there are still simple-looking languages that fall outside this class.

We start, however, with a mechanism to generate strings, called a grammar. Grammars were originally invented to describe features of human spoken languages. They have proved useful as a way to describe computer languages, and even as a programming tool. Our main focus here is on a special type of grammar, known as a context-free grammar.

Language is a form of human reason, which has its internal logic of which man knows nothing. **—Claude Levi-Strauss**

It is of interest to note that while some dolphins are reported to have learned English—up to fifty words used in correct context—no human being has been reported to have learned dolphinese. **—Carl Sagan**

I don't want to talk grammar, I want to talk like a lady.
—George Bernard Shaw, Pygmalion

Colorless green ideas sleep furiously. **—Noam Chomsky**

chapter

6

Context-Free Grammars

A grammar for a computer language is much like that for a natural language: a set of rules for putting things together. Each grammar corresponds to a language. Our focus is on a special type of grammar, called a context-free grammar.

6.1 Productions

This is an example of a context-free grammar:

Example 6.1	$S \to 0S1$ $S \to \varepsilon$

A **grammar** consists of

- A set of **variables** (also called nonterminals)
- A set of **terminals** (from the alphabet)
- A list of **productions** (also called rules)

In the preceding example, S is the only variable. The terminals are 0 and 1. There are two productions. It is customary to use upper-case letters for variables.

How does a grammar work? A production allows you to take a string containing a variable and replace the variable by the right-hand side of the production. We say that a (finite) string w, consisting of terminals, is **generated** by the grammar if, starting with the start variable S, you can apply productions and end up with that string. The sequence of strings so obtained is called a **derivation** of w. We will see later other versions of a grammar; this version is called a **context-free grammar** (CFG). A language is **context-free** if it is generated by a CFG.

Example 6.1 (continued)

The string 0011 is in the language generated. The derivation is:

$$S \Longrightarrow 0S1 \Longrightarrow 00S11 \Longrightarrow 0011$$

The first two steps use the first production; the final step uses the second production.

What does this language contain? Certainly every string generated has an equal number of 0's and 1's. In fact, it is our nonregular language $\{\, 0^n 1^n : n \geq 0 \,\}$.

Notice that a CFG has a **recursive** flavor about it. In the preceding example, the CFG says that all strings in the language can be built up starting with the empty string and repeatedly wrapping with the symbols 0 and 1. Without recursion, the grammar would only define a finite language.

As for notation, we could also write the preceding CFG as

$$S \rightarrow 0S1 \mid \varepsilon$$

where the vertical bar means *or*.

Example 6.2

We saw earlier that the language P of palindromes with alphabet $\{a, b\}$ is nonregular. We can determine a CFG for it by finding a recursive decomposition. If you peel the first and last symbols from a palindrome, what remains is a palindrome; and if you wrap a palindrome with the same symbol in front and in back, then it is still a palindrome. This is the basis for the following CFG:

$$P \rightarrow aPa \mid bPb \mid \varepsilon$$

Actually, this generates all palindromes of even length. An exercise asks how to adapt this CFG to generate all palindromes.

Mathematicians might write the language of even-length palindromes as $\{\, w w^R : w \in \Sigma^* \,\}$.

We can provide a **formal definition** of a context-free grammar. It is a 4-tuple (V, Σ, S, P) where:

- V is a finite set of variables.
- Σ is a finite alphabet of terminals.
- S is the start variable.
- P is the finite set of productions. Each production has the form $V \to (V \cup \Sigma)^*$.

6.2 Further Examples

We start with CFGs for some regular languages.

Example 6.3

A CFG for all binary strings with an even number of 0's.

Well, how to decompose such a string? If the first symbol is a 1, then an even number of 0's remains. If the first symbol is a 0, then go to the next 0; what remains after that symbol is again a string with an even number of 0's. This yields the following CFG:

$$S \to 1S \mid 0A0S \mid \varepsilon$$
$$A \to 1A \mid \varepsilon$$

But a language can have more than one grammar. For example, when the first symbol is a 0, you might also observe that what remains has an odd number of 0's. If we use T to generate all binary strings with an odd number of 0's, we get the following CFG:

$$S \to 1S \mid 0T \mid \varepsilon$$
$$T \to 1T \mid 0S$$

Example 6.4

A CFG for the regular language corresponding to the RE 00*11*.

The idea is that the language is the concatenation of two languages: the first language is all strings of 0's, and the second is all strings of 1's.

$$S \to CD$$
$$C \to 0C \mid 0$$
$$D \to 1D \mid 1$$

The next example is the complement of the language from the previous example. There is no obvious way to convert a grammar to its complement. The goal here is a CFG for all strings *not* of the form $0^i 1^j$ where $i, j > 0$. One approach is to partition the set of strings into the three failures:

- String not of the right form: somewhere there is a 1 followed by a 0
- Only zeroes
- Only ones

This yields the following CFG.

Example 6.5   **Complement of $\{\, 0^i 1^j : i, j > 0 \,\}$.**

$$S \rightarrow A \mid B \mid C$$
$$A \rightarrow D\,10\,D$$
$$D \rightarrow 0D \mid 1D \mid \varepsilon$$
$$B \rightarrow 0B \mid 0$$
$$C \rightarrow 1C \mid 1$$

The variable A will produce all strings with a 0 and 1 out of order, variable B will produce strings of zeroes, variable C will produce strings of ones, and variable D will produce all strings.

Note that to check that a grammar and a description match, you must check two things: that everything the grammar generates fits the description (sometimes called **consistency**), and that everything in the description is generated by the grammar (sometimes called **completeness**).

Example 6.6   Consider the CFG

$$S \rightarrow 0S\,1S \mid 1S\,0S \mid \varepsilon$$

The string 011100 is in the language generated by the preceding grammar. One derivation is the following:

$$S \Longrightarrow 0S\,1S \Longrightarrow 01S \Longrightarrow 011S\,0S \Longrightarrow 0111S\,0S\,0S \Longrightarrow 01110S\,0S$$
$$\Longrightarrow 011100S \Longrightarrow 011100$$

What does this language contain? Certainly, every string generated has an equal number of 0's and 1's. But can any string with an equal number of 0's and 1's be generated? Yes. Why?

Well, whatever the string starts with, at some point, equality between the numbers of symbols must be reached. The key point is that if the string starts with a 0, then the first time equality is reached is at a 1. Then the portion of the string between the first symbol and this 1 is itself an example of equality, as is the portion after this 1. That is, you can break up the string as $0w1x$, where both strings w and x belong to the language. For example, here is the breakup of 00101101:

$$0 \; \boxed{0 \; 1 \; 0 \; 1} \; 1 \; \boxed{0 \; 1}$$
$$ w x$$

This argument shows the completeness: every string with an equal number of zeroes and ones is generated.

Grammars originally arose in the study of human languages. For example, here is a primitive grammar that generates sentences as composed of noun and verb phrases:

Example 6.7

$$S \rightarrow NP \; VP$$
$$NP \rightarrow \text{the } N$$
$$VP \rightarrow V \; N$$
$$V \rightarrow \text{sings} \mid \text{eats}$$
$$N \rightarrow \text{cat} \mid \text{song} \mid \text{canary}$$

This generates "the canary sings the song", but also "the song eats the cat".

The above CFG generates all "legal" sentences, not just those that are meaningful.

6.3 Derivation Trees and Ambiguity

For strings α and β, we say α **yields** β, written $\alpha \stackrel{*}{\Longrightarrow} \beta$ if it is possible to get from α to β using the productions. A **derivation** of β is the sequence of steps that gets to β. A **leftmost** derivation is where at each stage one replaces the leftmost variable. In Example 6.6, the derivation of 011100 that is given is a leftmost derivation. A **rightmost derivation** is defined similarly.

You can also represent the derivation by a **derivation tree**. The root of the tree is the designated start variable, all internal nodes are labeled with variables, while the leaves are labeled with terminals. The children of a node are labeled from left to right with the right-hand side of the production used. There is a 1-to-1 correspondence between derivation trees, leftmost derivations, and rightmost derivations.

| Example 6.8 | The derivation tree for the string `011100` in the grammar of Example 6.6 is drawn: |

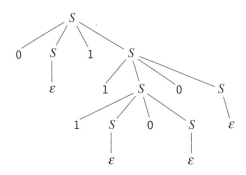

We say that a grammar is **unambiguous** if there is a unique leftmost derivation for each string in the language. Equivalently, for each string in the language there is a unique derivation tree. For example, the grammar in Example 6.6 is ambiguous—but not for the example string. (The string `0101` has two derivation trees—find them.)

Grammars are used in compilers. A compiler checks that the input file or expression is valid by essentially finding the derivation tree. This derivation tree is then used in finding code for the file or expression. If the grammar is unambiguous, the derivation tree is always unique. This process is discussed in Chapter 10.

| Example 6.9 | The language of arithmetical expressions using only multiplication and addition can be described as the following with start variable E: |

$$E \rightarrow E + T \mid T$$
$$T \rightarrow T \times F \mid F$$
$$F \rightarrow (E) \mid number$$

(Think of Expression, Factor, and Term.) This generates expressions such as 1+(3+2)×5 and 1+2×3. The derivation tree for the latter is as follows.

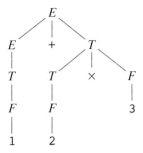

Note that the derivation tree automatically knows that multiplication takes precedence over addition.

6.4 Regular Languages Revisited

What is the relationship between regular languages and context-free languages? The following is probably not surprising.

Theorem	Every regular language is generated by a context-free grammar.

Proof	One way to prove this is to convert an RE to a CFG. This can be achieved recursively. For example, if the overall language is the union of two pieces, you can write $S \rightarrow A \mid B$; and if it is the concatenation of two pieces, you can write $S \rightarrow CD$. If the overall language is the star of a piece, say, generated by E, then you can write $S \rightarrow ES \mid \varepsilon$. ◆

Example 6.10	Consider the RE $(11 + 00)^*11$. At the top level, it is the *concatenation* of two pieces. The first piece is the *or* of two parts. This yields the following grammar:

$$S \rightarrow TU$$
$$U \rightarrow 11$$
$$T \rightarrow TV$$
$$V \rightarrow 00 \mid 11$$

**For You
to Do!**

Give grammars for the following two languages:

1. All binary strings with both an even number of zeroes and an even number of ones.
2. All strings of the form $0^a 1^b 0^c$ such that $a + c = b$. (Hint: It's the concatenation of two simpler languages.)

EXERCISES

6.1 Give a CFG for palindromes that allows odd-length palindromes.

6.2 Construct a CFG for the language of binary strings of the form $0^n 1^{2n}$.

6.3 For each of the following CFGs: (1) determine which of the strings ε, abba, aaaaa, and b is generated, and (2) give an English description of the language.

   a) $S \to \mathsf{a}S \mid \mathsf{b}S \mid \mathsf{a} \mid \mathsf{b} \mid \varepsilon$

   b) $S \to X\,\mathsf{aaa}\,X$
      $X \to \mathsf{a}X \mid \mathsf{b}X \mid \varepsilon$

   c) $S \to \mathsf{aa}S \mid \mathsf{aaa}S \mid \mathsf{a}$

   d) $S \to \mathsf{a}X \mid \mathsf{b}S \mid \mathsf{a} \mid \mathsf{b}$
      $X \to \mathsf{a}X \mid \mathsf{a}$

★ 6.4 Show that the set of context-free languages is closed under the three Kleene operators.

6.5 Give CFGs for all strings of the form:

   a) $1\,0^n\,1\,0^n\,1$

   b) $0^n 1^m 2^k$ with $n = m + k$

   c) $0^n 1^m 0^m 1^n$

   d) $0^i 1^j 2^k$ with $i = j$ or $i = k$

6.6 Give CFGs for the following languages with alphabet $\{\mathsf{a}, \mathsf{b}\}$:

   a) All strings of the form $\mathsf{a}^m \mathsf{b}^n$ with $m \le n \le 2m$.

   b) All strings such that the middle symbol is a.

6.7 Give a CFG for the complement of $\{0^n 1^n : n \ge 0\}$.

★ 6.8 In a string, a **block** is a substring, all of whose symbols are the same and which cannot be enlarged. For example, 0001100 has *three* blocks. Let L be the language consisting of all binary strings that have (somewhere) two blocks of zeroes of the same length. For example, $011001110 \in L$ and $11101011 \in L$, but $000110011 \notin L$. Give a grammar for L.

H **6.9** Construct a CFG for the language of binary strings with an unequal number of 0's and 1's.

6.10 Consider the following CFG with start variable S:

$$S \rightarrow BB$$
$$B \rightarrow SS \mid \mathtt{c}$$

    a) What is the shortest string in the language of the grammar?
    b) Draw the derivation tree for the string from (a).
    c) Is this grammar ambiguous? Explain.
    d) Describe in English the language generated by the grammar.
    e) Does this CFG generate a regular language? Explain.

6.11 Describe in English the language generated by the following grammar:

$$S \rightarrow 0S1 \mid 1S0 \mid \varepsilon \mid SS$$

Sketch a proof that your answer is correct.

★ **6.12** Explain what language this CFG generates (with start variable S):

$$S \rightarrow AB$$
$$A \rightarrow 0A1 \mid \varepsilon$$
$$B \rightarrow 1B0 \mid \varepsilon$$

Sketch a proof that your answer is correct.

6.13 Give the shortest string generated by the following CFG (with start variable S and alphabet $\{0, 1\}$), and give a derivation tree for that string:

$$S \rightarrow ABA \mid SS$$
$$A \rightarrow S0 \mid T1T$$
$$B \rightarrow S1 \mid 0$$
$$T \rightarrow 0$$

6.14 Consider the language L of all strings of a's and b's such that there are more a's than b's. Does the following grammar generate L? Justify your answer.

$$S \rightarrow \mathtt{a}S\mathtt{b} \mid \mathtt{b}S\mathtt{a} \mid S\mathtt{ba} \mid S\mathtt{ab} \mid \mathtt{ab}S \mid \mathtt{ba}S \mid \mathtt{a}S \mid S\mathtt{a} \mid \mathtt{a}$$

H **6.15** Consider the language D of all strings of a's and b's with twice as many a's as b's.

    a) Does the following grammar generate D? Justify your answer.

$$S \rightarrow \mathtt{a}S\mathtt{a}S\mathtt{b}S \mid \mathtt{a}S\mathtt{b}S\mathtt{a}S \mid \mathtt{b}S\mathtt{a}S\mathtt{a}S \mid \varepsilon$$

b) Does the following grammar generate D? Justify your answer.

$$S \rightarrow SS \mid AB \mid BA \mid \varepsilon$$
$$A \rightarrow AS \mid SA \mid \text{a}$$
$$B \rightarrow SB \mid BS \mid A\text{b} \mid \text{b}A$$

★ **6.16** Consider the grammar $S \rightarrow SS \mid SSS \mid \text{x}$.

    a) Draw all derivation trees for xxx.

    b) How many derivation trees are there for xxxx? Explain.

  6.17 For the CFGs in Exercise 6.3, determine which are ambiguous, and for each of those, find a string that shows that the CFG is ambiguous.

  6.18 Let G be a CFG in which every variable occurs on the left-hand side of at most one production. Prove that G is unambiguous.

  6.19 Consider a programming language Puny that allows only a few things. These include declaration of **int** variables; assignments where the right-hand side uses only operators, variables, and constants; a **begin** only at the beginning of a program and **end** at the end; all declarations at the start; and all statements ending with a semicolon. There is also a loop construct that can be nested.

    a) Derive a grammar.

    b) Sketch the parse tree for the following code. (The tree is huge! So draw it in pieces.)

```
begin
  int x; int y;
  while x!=y :
    x = x+1;
    while x!=0 :
        y = y*x + 22;
    endwhile;
  endwhile;
end
```

★ **6.20** Give a CFG for the language R where R is the set of all REs with alphabet $\{\text{a}, \text{b}\}$.

"For You to Do" Exercise Solutions

1. $S \rightarrow 0X \mid 1Y \mid \varepsilon$

    $X \rightarrow 0S \mid 1Z$ (odd zeroes, even ones)

    $Y \rightarrow 1S \mid 0Z$ (odd ones, even zeroes)

    $Z \rightarrow 0Y \mid 1X$ (odd ones, odd zeroes)

2. $S \rightarrow TU$

    $T \rightarrow 0T1 \mid \varepsilon$

    $U \rightarrow 1U0 \mid \varepsilon$

chapter

7

Pushdown Automata

$\mathbf{W}$e consider now a model of a computer that is more powerful than a finite automaton. In this model, we give the FA some memory; in particular, we give it a stack.

7.1 A PDA Has a Stack

A stack is a way of storing information on a last-in, first-out principle. Everything that is added to a stack is added to the top, and everything that is removed from the stack is removed from the top. There is always only one exposed item. The process of adding an item to the stack is called pushing; the item goes on the top. The process of removing an item from the stack is called popping; the item removed was the top item.

A pushdown automaton (PDA) is like an FA in that there is a fixed finite number of states that it can be. But it also has one unbounded stack for storage. A PDA works by reading the input. When a symbol is read, depending on

a) the state of the machine,
b) the symbol on top of the stack, and
c) the symbol read,

the machine

1. updates its state, and
2. pops or pushes a symbol.

The machine may also pop or push without reading input.

We draw the **program** of a PDA as a **flowchart**. There are five components to this:

- A single **start** state
- A single **halt-and-accept** state
- A **reader** box: this reads one symbol from the input and, depending on the symbol read, goes to a new state (just as in an FA)
- A **pop** box: this pops one symbol from the stack and, depending on the symbol, goes to a new state
- A **push** box: this adds a specific symbol to the stack

Note that the flowchart has no reject state. Rather, if the machine gets to a state and there is no legal continuation, then *we assume the machine halts and rejects the input.*

We also need a **special symbol**: we will use Δ to indicate the end of the input string. We will also use Δ to indicate the result of popping when the stack is empty—you could also think of this as the stack starting with the special symbol Δ on it.

Example 7.1

The language $\{\, 0^n 1^n : n > 0 \,\}$. (See Example 6.1.)

The PDA will use the stack as a counter. The machine starts with an empty stack. As a symbol comes in, the machine checks whether it is a 0. If so, it pushes an x onto the stack. When the first 1 is encountered, the machine enters a new state. In this state, it pops symbols off the stack, one for each input 1. If, during this phase, a 0 is encountered or the stack becomes empty, then the machine rejects the string (because either the string doesn't have the right form or there are too few 1's). The PDA accepts if and only if the stack becomes empty at the same time the end of the string is reached.

The PDA is shown in Figure 7.1. To get a feel for it, walk through this PDA with the strings 000111, 0010, and 011. (Some would prefer to push 0's rather than x's onto the stack.)

Casualness   There are traditional shapes for the different types of functions on the flowchart—diamonds for decisions based on reading or popping, rectangles for pushes, and lozenges for start and accept states—but don't worry too much about that. Also, the empty string often requires very special handling; from now on, however, we will simply *ignore the empty string.*

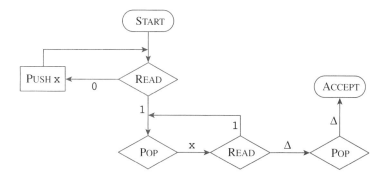

Figure 7.1   A PDA for $0^n 1^n$

Balanced brackets.

We consider here strings consisting entirely of left and right brackets. Such a string is called **balanced** if (a) reading from left to right the number of left brackets is always at least the number of right brackets; and (b) the total number of left brackets equals the total number of right brackets. For example,

$\quad(\,(\,)\,(\,)\,)\,(\,)\quad$ is balanced; $(\,(\,)$ and $)\,)\,)\,($ are not.

In a normal arithmetical expression, the brackets are always balanced.

It is easy to produce a grammar for such strings:

$$S \to (S) \mid SS \mid \varepsilon$$

In the PDA for such strings, each opening bracket (is simply pushed; each closing bracket) causes a matching (to be popped. The PDA is drawn in Figure 7.2.

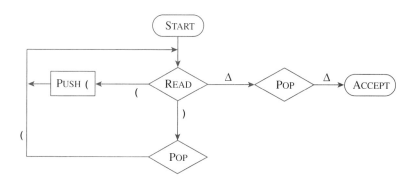

Figure 7.2   A PDA for balanced brackets

7.2 Nondeterminism and Further Examples

What about a PDA for palindromes? What we do is use nondeterminism. In fact, *by definition*, a PDA is nondeterministic. We say that the PDA accepts the input string if **there exists** a sequence of actions that leads to the accept state. There are two ways to depict nondeterminism in the flowchart: there can be two transitions with the same label, or there can be a transition labeled with ε (which does not consume an input symbol).

So what about a PDA for palindromes? Well, you read the input and stack it away merrily. Until suddenly you have this premonition that the middle of the road has been reached. Then, you start popping, each time checking that the input symbol matches the one on the stack. If ever there is a conflict, the machine dies gracefully. If the input ends before the stack is empty, or the stack is empty before the input ends, then again it dies. The machine accepts the string if it reaches the empty stack at the end of the input and never encounters a conflict. This PDA is shown in Figure 7.3.

It can be proven that you need nondeterminism for palindromes.

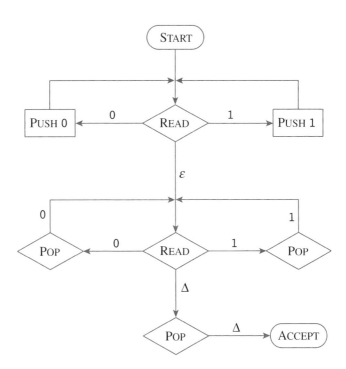

Figure 7.3   A PDA for even-length palindromes

Here is another language that benefits from nondeterminism.

Example 7.3 **The language $\{\, 0^m 1^n : n \leq m \leq 2n \,\}$.**

The first phase should be clear: you need to count the number of zeroes. Say we use the stack symbol x like we did with $0^n 1^n$. After that, we want to match zeroes with ones. Actually, to make this work, it is sufficient to match each 1 with either one or two x's. You can guess when to do the change over, or you can simply intermingle the matches, allowing the nondeterminism to choose the correct path. The PDA with the former approach is drawn in Figure 7.4.

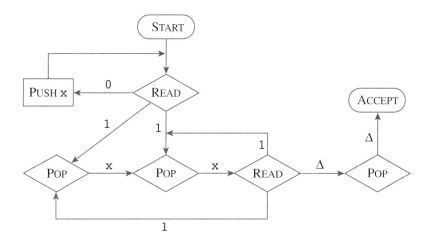

Figure 7.4   A PDA for $\{0^m 1^n : n \leq m \leq 2n\}$

The next PDA is for all binary strings with an **equal number of 0's and 1's**. The idea is to use the stack as a counter, but the details can be a bit complex. It is natural that the stack keeps track of the difference between the number of 0's and 1's so far. The key idea to get a simple PDA is to store 0's on the stack if the 0's are in the majority, and to store 1's if the 1's are in the majority.

The PDA is shown in Figure 7.5. How does it work? Consider the leftmost read state. The invariant is that whenever here, the 0's are in the majority, and the stack has *one less* 0 than the excess (so the stack is empty when the 0's outnumber the 1's by only one). We are at the middle read state whenever there have been equal numbers of the two symbols.

We defer the formal definition of a PDA until the next chapter because there is an alternative representation that is more in line with the formal definition.

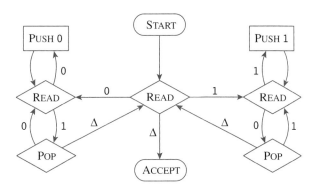

Figure 7.5   A PDA for equal 0's and 1's

7.3 Context-Free Languages

The big theorem (if you hadn't guessed it by now) is as follows.

Theorem	A language is generated by a context-free grammar if and only if it is accepted by a pushdown automaton.

We prove the theorem in the next chapter. It follows that a context-free language is one that is generated by a CFG or accepted by a PDA.

7.4 Applications of PDAs

Pushdown automata are useful in compilers. For example, an arithmetical expression can be first understood using a stack, and then evaluated using a stack, as the following example shows.

Example 7.4   Recall the CFG for arithmetic from Example 6.9. A postorder traversal of the derivation tree provides what is called the **reverse Polish** form of the expression. This can be used to provide code for evaluation using a stack.

For example, if MUL is a function to replace the top two values on the stack by their product, and ADD replaces the top two values on the stack by their sum, an expression evaluator might convert

$$1 + 5 * (3 + 2) + 4$$

into the code

PUSH(1) PUSH(5) PUSH(3) PUSH(2) ADD MUL ADD PUSH(4) ADD

For You to Do!

1. Draw a PDA for the set of all strings of the form $0^a 1^b$ such that $a \geq b$.
2. Draw a PDA for the set of all strings of the form $0^a 1^b 0^c$ such that $a + c = b$.

EXERCISES

7.1 Adapt the PDA from Figure 7.3 to accept odd-length palindromes as well.

7.2 Construct a PDA for the language of strings of the form $0^n 1^{2n}$.

7.3 Construct a PDA for the language of strings of the form $0^n 1 0^n$.

★ **7.4** Construct a PDA for strings that consist of three parts, where the first part is a binary string, the second part is the symbol #, and the third part is the reverse of the first part. For example, 01001#10010 is in the language.

7.5 Walk through the silly PDA in Figure 7.6 with the strings abba, babab, and baaa. What language does it accept?

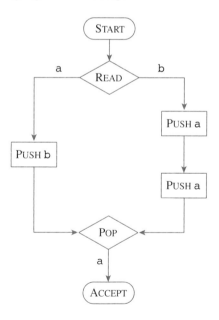

Figure 7.6 A silly PDA

7.6 Explain how, given a PDA for L_1 and a PDA for L_2, you can produce a PDA for the concatenation $L_1 L_2$.

H **7.7** Give a PDA for all binary strings that are *not* of the form ww.

★ **7.8** Give a PDA for the language $\{\, 0^m\, 1^n : m = n \text{ or } m = 2n \,\}$.

7.9 Construct a PDA for the language of binary strings with an unequal number of 0's and 1's.

7.10 Consider the following (nondeterministic) PDA.

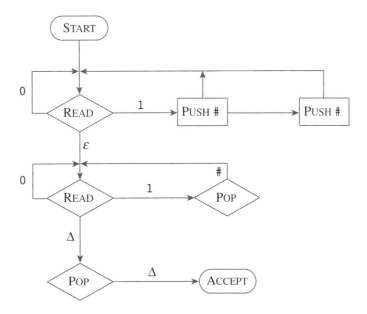

  a) List **three** strings the PDA accepts.

  b) Describe in English the language accepted by the machine.

7.11 Construct PDAs for the languages of Exercise 6.5.

★ **7.12** Construct PDAs for the languages of Exercise 6.6.

7.13 Consider the language of strings where (at least) the first half is all the same symbol. To be specific, consider the set of all strings $a^n x$ where $|x| \le n$ and $x \in \{a, b\}^*$. Give both a grammar and a PDA for this language.

7.14 Suppose M_1 is a PDA for language L_1 and M_2 is a PDA for language L_2. Explain how to build a PDA for the language $L_1 \cup L_2$.

7.15 Construct a PDA for the language of Exercise 6.7.

★ **7.16** Describe in English a PDA for the language of Exercise 6.8.

7.17 Describe in English a PDA accepting the language L as follows:

> $L = \{\, w_1 \# w_2 \# \ldots \# w_k \# w : w, w_i \in \{0, 1\}^*, \text{ and } w_j = w^R \text{ for some } j \,\}$. That is, for a string to be in L, it must have alphabet a subset of $\{0, 1, \#\}$, and when cut up into pieces by omitting the #, the final piece is the reverse of one of the other pieces.

7.18 Consider the following description of a PDA. Draw the PDA as a flowchart, and explain in English what this PDA accepts:

> Until you reach the end of the input do the following: if a 1 is read, then push it; and if a 0 is read, then pop, checking that the stack does not underflow. When the end of the input is reached, accept provided the stack is not empty.

7.19 Convince your dog that a PDA can do anything an FA can do.

"For You to Do" Exercise Solutions

1.

2.

chapter

8

Grammars and Equivalences

In this chapter, we consider the Chomsky hierarchy, which includes more specific and more general grammars than context-free grammars. We also provide the proof that CFGs and PDAs have the same power.

8.1 Regular Grammars

We noted earlier that every regular language has a CFG. In fact, a regular language (without the empty string) can be generated by a grammar of a special form called a **regular grammar**. This is a grammar in which every production is of the form $A \to bC$ or $A \to a$ (where a and b are arbitrary terminals and C is an arbitrary variable).

Theorem	Every regular language is generated by a regular grammar.

Proof	The idea is to produce a grammar such that a derivation of a string mimics the feeding of that string into the automaton. At every stage of the derivation there will be a single variable, and that variable will remember the state of the automaton.

In particular, proceed as follows. Start with the DFA for the language. Introduce one variable for each state. For each transition, add a production: if $\delta(A, x) = B$, then add the production $A \to xB$. For each transition ending at an accept state, add a further production: if B is an accept state in the preceding, then also add the production $A \rightarrow$ x. The start variable is the start state.

♦

We illustrate the theorem with an example FA. Actually, an NFA is fine, but adding ε-transitions makes the process a bit muddier, so we do one without.

Example 8.1   Here is the construction of the regular grammar for the language of the RE $(11 + 00)^*11$.

Here is an NFA for the language:

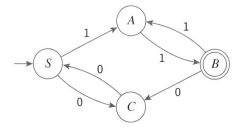

This yields the following regular grammar:

$$S \rightarrow 0C \mid 1A$$
$$A \rightarrow 1B \mid 1$$
$$B \rightarrow 0C \mid 1A$$
$$C \rightarrow 0S$$

 For You to Do!

1. Draw an FA, and from there write down a regular grammar for the language given by the RE 00^*11^* (first considered in Example 6.4).

8.2   The Chomsky Hierarchy

In his study of natural languages, Chomsky introduced a hierarchy of grammars. These allow for productions of various types:

0. **Unrestricted grammars.** Productions have the form $u \rightarrow v$ where u and v are any strings of terminals and/or variables.

1. **Context-sensitive grammars.** Productions have the form $xAz \rightarrow xyz$, where x, y, and z are strings of terminals and/or variables, and A is a variable. This means that A can be replaced, provided it is correctly surrounded; that is, it is in the correct context.
2. **Context-free grammars.** Productions have the form $A \rightarrow v$, where A is a variable and v a string.
3. **Regular grammars.** Productions have the form $A \rightarrow \text{b}C$ or $A \rightarrow \text{a}$, where a and b are terminals and A and C are variables.

We have seen that regular grammars are accepted by FAs, and that context-free grammars are accepted by PDAs. We will see later machines for the other two types of grammars.

Context-sensitive grammars are intricate affairs. Here is a famous example:

Example 8.2 | **A context-sensitive grammar for $0^n 1^n 2^n$.**

$$S \rightarrow 0BS2 \mid 012$$
$$B0 \rightarrow 0B$$
$$B1 \rightarrow 11$$

See if you can provide the derivation for 000111222.

8.3 Usable and Nullable Variables

It will be useful to manipulate grammars, especially to simplify them. Two ideas that arise are usable and nullable variables. A variable is said to be **usable** if it produces some string of terminals. A variable is said to be **nullable** if the empty string is one of the strings it generates.

Example 8.3 | In the following grammar, A and B are usable, but only B is nullable.

$$A \rightarrow 0A \mid 1B \mid 2C$$
$$B \rightarrow 0B \mid \varepsilon$$
$$C \rightarrow 1C$$

There is an algorithm for determining if a variable in a CFG is nullable. Indeed, the algorithm determines all nullable variables.

Identification of nullable variables	Initialize all variables as not-nullable.
	Repeat:
	Go through all productions, and if any has right-hand side empty or all entries nullable, Then mark the left-hand side variable as nullable
	Until there is no increase in the set of nullable variables.

A similar procedure can be used to determine the usable variables, but we leave it as an exercise.

8.4 Conversion from CFG to PDA

We turn next to proving the theorem that a language is generated by a context-free grammar if and only if it is accepted by a pushdown automaton. The proof consists of two conversions. We start with the conversion from CFG to PDA.

The basic idea in going from a CFG to a PDA is that the PDA guesses the leftmost derivation and then checks that it is correct. This is a **proof by simulation**.

For example, we gave in Example 6.6 a leftmost derivation of the string 011100. Each step of the derivation is a string. The machine guesses the next step. The problem is to do this with only a stack for storage.

The idea is that terminals to the left of the leftmost variable do not have to be stored; instead they can be matched with the input string. The portion of the current string from the leftmost variable onward is then stored on the stack, with the *leftmost* symbol on top.

The PDA works as follows. It begins with the start variable on the stack. At each step, the PDA looks at the top of the stack:

- If there is a variable on the top, the PDA guesses a production and replaces the variable by the right-hand side of that production.
- If there is a terminal on the top, then the PDA pops it and reads one symbol from the input string and checks that the two match. (If not, this branch dies.)

When the stack is empty, the machine then checks that the input string is finished. If so, it accepts; else, it dies. Note that the machine is not guaranteed to halt.

For example, consider the CFG of Example 6.6 that generates all binary strings with an equal number of 0's and 1's. The sequence of stacks for the accepting branch of the PDA for the string 011100 starts as follows:

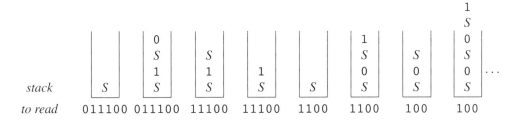

stack

to read   011100 011100 11100 11100 1100 1100 100 100

8.5   An Alternative Representation

We show next how to convert from a PDA to a CFG. This procedure is slightly easier if the PDA is in another form, where only the reading states are retained and the stack operations become part of the transitions.

Example 8.4   Consider our first PDA, given in Figure 7.1. That PDA has essentially three states: if we let F denote the first READ, let G denote the second READ, and let H denote the final accept state, then we get the following diagram for the PDA:

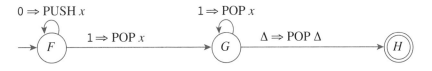

In this light, we can also provide a **formal definition** of a PDA. Specifically, a pushdown automaton is a 7-tuple $(Q, \Sigma, \Gamma, q_0, h_a, \Delta, \delta)$ where:

- Q is a finite set of states.
- Σ is the finite input alphabet.
- Γ is the finite stack alphabet.
- q_0 is the start state.
- h_a is the accept state.
- Δ is the empty-stack and end-of-string symbol.
- δ is the transition function.

The transition function is a function from $Q \times (\Gamma \cup \{\Delta\}) \times (\Sigma \cup \{\varepsilon, \Delta\})$ to finite subsets of $Q \times \Gamma^*$. That is, it looks at the current state, at the current symbol on top of the stack, and possibly at the input symbol, and then proceeds to update the state and replace the current symbol on top of the stack by a string of symbols. In this formulation,

> *A pop is equivalent to replacing the stack-top symbol by nothing.*
>
> *A push is equivalent to replacing the stack-top symbol by itself and a new symbol.*

For example, $\delta(q, \mathtt{A}, \mathtt{a}) = \{(p, \mathtt{AB})\}$ means that in state q with $\mathtt{A}$ on top of the stack, on reading $\mathtt{a}$ the machine should push symbol $\mathtt{B}$ and change to state p.

8.6   Conversion from PDA to CFG

The idea for the conversion from PDA to CFG is to make each step in a derivation correspond to a move by the PDA. This is not trivial!

We use the alternative representation from the previous section. It helps to modify the machine further. Specifically, we assume that the stack of the PDA M is empty if and only if M is in the accept state. Further, we assume that every move is either a push of a single symbol or a pop of a single symbol (changing state while doing neither is not allowed). It is left as an exercise to show that you can massage a PDA into this form.

The variables of the CFG will be *all* the ordered triples $\boxed{q\,\mathtt{A}\,p}$ where q, p are states of the PDA, and $\mathtt{A}$ is a symbol from the stack alphabet. The aim is to construct the grammar such that for all strings w:

$$\boxed{q\,A\,p} \overset{*}{\Longrightarrow} w \quad \Leftrightarrow \quad \begin{array}{l} \textit{M can go from state q to state p while} \\ \textit{reading string w with the net effect of} \\ \textit{popping the symbol A from the stack.} \end{array}$$

If q_0 is the start state and h_a is the accept state of M, then $[q_0, \Delta, h_a]$ will be the start variable for the CFG: it will generate string w if and only if it is possible to go from q_0 to h_a while reading w and popping the empty-stack symbol; that is, w is accepted.

The moves of the PDA are converted to productions. There are two possible moves of the PDA, push and pop. Consider a **pop** move. Say $(p, \varepsilon) \in \delta(q, \mathtt{A}, \mathtt{a})$. That is, in state q it is possible to pop symbol $\mathtt{A}$ while reading $\mathtt{a}$ and changing to state p. Here, $\mathtt{a}$ is either a symbol from the input alphabet or the empty string ε. Then we simply add the production:

$$\boxed{q\,A\,p} \to \mathtt{a}$$

Consider a **push** move. Say $(p, \text{AB}) \in \delta(q, \text{A}, \text{a})$. That is, in state q with A on top of the stack it is possible to push symbol B while reading a and changing to state p. Then we add the collection of productions:

$$\boxed{q\,A\,r} \;\to\; \text{a} \;\boxed{p\,B\,s}\;\boxed{s\,A\,r} \qquad \text{for every state } r \text{ and } s$$

What this says is that there are two ways to effectively erase the symbol on top of the stack. The first is to pop it; the second is to push something, and then later erase both symbols.

The rest of the proof is to show that every derivation in this grammar corresponds to a legitimate computation of the PDA. We omit the (lengthy) details.

Example 8.5

Here is an example conversion from PDA to CFG. We include this more as evidence that the method actually works rather than seriously proposing you learn how to do this. . . .

We use the PDA for $\{0^n 1^n\}$ from Example 8.4. Here goes . . .

Start symbol: $\boxed{F\,\Delta\,H}$

Popping occurs in three places:

$$\boxed{F\,\text{x}\,G} \;\to\; 1$$

$$\boxed{G\,\text{x}\,G} \;\to\; 1$$

$$\boxed{G\,\Delta\,H} \;\to\; \varepsilon$$

Pushing yields 18 productions of the form

$$\boxed{F\,A\,r} \;\to\; 0\;\boxed{F\,\text{x}\,s}\;\boxed{s\,A\,r} \qquad \text{for each } A \in \{\text{x}, \Delta\} \text{ and}$$
$$r, s \in \{F, G, H\}.$$

Now note that only eight triples ever occur on the left-hand side (including six $\boxed{F\,?\,?}$). So, we can omit those productions that produce unusable triples to yield the following list:

1. $\boxed{F\,\text{x}\,F} \;\to\; 0\;\boxed{F\,\text{x}\,F}\;\boxed{F\,\text{x}\,F}$

2. $\boxed{F \times G} \to 0 \boxed{F \times F} \boxed{F \times G}$

3. $\boxed{F \times H} \to 0 \boxed{F \times F} \boxed{F \times H}$

4. $\boxed{F \triangle F} \to 0 \boxed{F \times F} \boxed{F \triangle F}$

5. $\boxed{F \triangle G} \to 0 \boxed{F \times F} \boxed{F \triangle G}$

6. $\boxed{F \triangle H} \to 0 \boxed{F \times F} \boxed{F \triangle H}$

7. $\boxed{F \times G} \to 0 \boxed{F \times G} \boxed{G \times G}$

8. $\boxed{F \triangle H} \to 0 \boxed{F \times G} \boxed{G \triangle H}$

But now, notice that any production with left-hand side $\boxed{F \times F}$ produces a right-hand side with $\boxed{F \times F}$ in it. And so you cannot get rid of this variable once it is introduced into a derivation. That is, all of productions 1 through 6 are of no use.

This leaves us with the CFG with start variable $\boxed{F \triangle H}$:

$\boxed{F \times G} \to 1$

$\boxed{G \times G} \to 1$

$\boxed{G \triangle H} \to \varepsilon$

$\boxed{F \times G} \to 0 \boxed{F \times G} \boxed{G \times G}$

$\boxed{F \triangle H} \to 0 \boxed{F \times G} \boxed{G \triangle H}$

Whew!

EXERCISES

8.1 Let L be the language corresponding to the RE b(ab)*. For the following CFG for L, determine the number of derivation trees for the string bababab.

$$S \to SaS \mid b$$

8.2 Give a regular grammar for L of the previous exercise.

8.3 Give a regular grammar for the language of the following FA (originally given in Example 1.1):

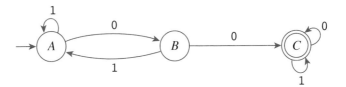

★ **8.4** Can a regular grammar be ambiguous? Explain.

8.5 Give a context-sensitive grammar for the language $\{\, \mathsf{a}^i \mathsf{b}^{2i} \mathsf{a}^i \,\}$.

Ⓗ **8.6** Give a context-sensitive grammar for the language $\{\, xx : x \in \{\mathsf{a},\mathsf{b}\}^* \,\}$.

8.7 Explain how to convert a PDA into the correct form for the proof of conversion to a CFG.

★ **8.8** Give a PDA equivalent to the following grammar:

$$S \to \mathsf{a}AA$$
$$A \to \mathsf{a}S \mid \mathsf{b}S \mid \mathsf{a}$$

8.9 Consider the PDA from Example 7.2 (balanced brackets).

  a) In the spirit of the diagram given in Example 8.4, draw a state-based diagram for it.

  b) Give the parts of this PDA in terms of the formal definition.

8.10 Suppose the stack of the PDA for language L never grows beyond 100 entries on any input. Show that L is regular.

8.11 A **2-PDA** is like a PDA except that it has two stacks.

  a) Show that the language $\{\, 0^n 1^n 2^n : n \geq 0 \,\}$ can be recognized by a 2-PDA.

  b) Show that the language $\{\, 0^n 1^n 2^n 3^n : n \geq 0 \,\}$ can be recognized by a 2-PDA.

  c) Show that the language $\{\, x\#x : x \in \{0,1\}^* \,\}$ can be recognized by a 2-PDA.

★ **8.12** Describe an algorithm to determine which variables in a CFG are usable. Hence, give an algorithm to determine whether the language of a CFG is empty or not.

"For You to Do" Exercise Solutions

1.

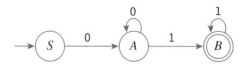

$$S \to 0A$$
$$A \to 0A \mid 1B \mid 1$$
$$B \to 1B \mid 1$$

chapter

9

Properties of Context-Free Languages

When showing the limits of regular languages, we introduced the Pumping Lemma. A similar Pumping Lemma is the tool to show a language is not context-free. In this chapter, we also consider properties of, and how to answer questions about, context-free languages.

9.1 Chomsky Normal Form

If a context-free language does not contain ε, then the grammar can be rewritten in Chomsky Normal Form and there is a simple (but sometimes tedious) algorithm for putting it in that form. There is also another normal form from Greibach (defined in Exercise 9.20). These normal forms can simplify matters in proving or calculating things about a grammar.

Chomsky Normal Form	A grammar where every production is either of the form $A \to BC$ or $A \to c$ (where A, B, C are arbitrary variables and c is an arbitrary symbol).

Example 9.1 The grammar

$$S \to AS \mid \text{a}$$
$$A \to SA \mid \text{b}$$

is in Chomsky Normal Form.

If the language contains the empty string, then it is standard to allow $S \to \varepsilon$ where S is the start symbol, and then forbid S on the right-hand side of any production. The key advantage is that in Chomsky Normal Form, every derivation of a string of n letters has exactly $2n - 1$ steps. Thus,

> *we can determine if a string is in the language by exhaustive search of all derivations.*

Slow but sure. We will see later that this can be speeded up.

The conversion to Chomsky Normal Form has four main steps:

1. *Get rid of all ε productions.* Recall that the nullable variables are those that generate the empty string; an algorithm for finding these was given earlier in Section 8.3. Determine the nullable variables. Then, go through all productions, and for each production omit every possible subset of nullable variables. For example, if one has production $P \to A\mathsf{x}B$ with both A and B nullable, then add the productions $P \to \mathsf{x}B \mid A\mathsf{x} \mid \mathsf{x}$. (If production P has k nullable variables on the right-hand side, then potentially $2^k - 1$ new productions are added.) After this, delete all the productions with empty right-hand sides.

2. *Get rid of all variable unit productions.* A unit production is one where the right-hand side has only one symbol. If you have the production $A \to B$, then for every production $B \to \alpha$, add the production $A \to \alpha$. Repeat until done (but don't re-create a unit production already deleted—you do have to be careful about chasing your tail).

3. *Replace every production that is too long by shorter productions.* For example, if you have the production $A \to BCD$, then replace it with $A \to BE$ and $E \to CD$. The process can be iterated with longer productions. (In theory, you introduce many new variables, but you can reuse variables if you are careful.)

4. *Move all terminals to unit productions.* For every terminal on the right of a nonunit production, add a substitute variable; for example, replace the production $A \to \mathsf{b}C$ with the productions $A \to BC$ and $B \to \mathsf{b}$.

Example 9.2   Consider the CFG:

$$S \to \mathsf{a}X\mathsf{b}X$$
$$X \to \mathsf{a}Y \mid \mathsf{b}Y \mid \varepsilon$$
$$Y \to X \mid \mathsf{c}$$

The variable X is nullable; and so therefore is Y. After elimination of ε we obtain:

$$S \to \mathtt{a}Xb X \mid \mathtt{ab}X \mid \mathtt{a}X\mathtt{b} \mid \mathtt{ab}$$
$$X \to \mathtt{a}Y \mid \mathtt{b}Y \mid \mathtt{a} \mid \mathtt{b}$$
$$Y \to X \mid \mathtt{c}$$

After elimination of the unit production $Y \to X$ we obtain:

$$S \to \mathtt{a}Xb X \mid \mathtt{ab}X \mid \mathtt{a}X\mathtt{b} \mid \mathtt{ab}$$
$$X \to \mathtt{a}Y \mid \mathtt{b}Y \mid \mathtt{a} \mid \mathtt{b}$$
$$Y \to \mathtt{a}Y \mid \mathtt{b}Y \mid \mathtt{a} \mid \mathtt{b} \mid \mathtt{c}$$

Now, we break up the right-hand sides of S. And we replace a by A, b by B, and c by C wherever they are not units (that is, where they appear with another symbol). So we obtain the following:

$$S \to EF \mid AF \mid EB \mid AB$$
$$X \to AY \mid BY \mid \mathtt{a} \mid \mathtt{b}$$
$$Y \to AY \mid BY \mid \mathtt{a} \mid \mathtt{b} \mid \mathtt{c}$$
$$E \to AX$$
$$F \to BX$$
$$A \to \mathtt{a}$$
$$B \to \mathtt{b}$$
$$C \to \mathtt{c}$$

(Whew!)

For You to Do!

1. Convert the following CFG into Chomsky Normal Form:

$$S \to A\mathtt{b}A$$
$$A \to A\mathtt{a} \mid \varepsilon$$

9.2 The Pumping Lemma: Proving Languages Not Context-Free

We saw that some languages cannot be recognized by FAs. Some languages cannot be recognized even by PDAs. One example is the language of all strings of the form $0^n 1^n 2^n$; that is, all strings of a number of 0's followed by an equal number of 1's followed by an equal number of 2's.

But to prove this we need a Pumping Lemma. This says that a context-free language has a certain repetitiveness about it.

Pumping Lemma

Let A be a context-free language. Then there is a constant number k such that, for every string $z \in A$ of length at least k, you can split z as $uvwxy$, where:

- ■ vx is nonempty
- ■ $|vwx| \leq k$
- ■ $uv^i wx^i y$ is in A for all $i \geq 0$

Proof

Assume A is generated by some CFG. Consider a very long string z in the language. Then, any derivation tree for z must have many leaves; in fact, it has $|z|$ leaves. Because there is an upper bound on the number of children a node can have, this means that the tree must be very deep—there must be a long path from the root to some leaf. So, if we make z long enough, there must be a path in the tree from S to a leaf that contains the same variable twice.

Suppose that variable is T. The leaves of the subtree under the second T form a string generated by T; call this string w. The leaves of the subtree under the first T form a string containing w; let v be the substring before w and x the substring after w. Finally, the leaves of the whole tree form the whole string z, which contains vwx; let u be the substring before vwx and y the substring after.

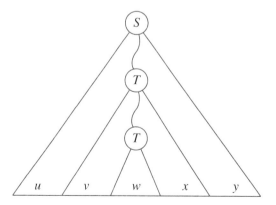

This means the following derivations hold: that $T \overset{*}{\Longrightarrow} w$, that $T \overset{*}{\Longrightarrow} vTx$, and that $S \overset{*}{\Longrightarrow} uTy$.

From this it follows that $T \overset{*}{\Rightarrow} v^i w x^i$ for all $i \geq 0$, and so $S \overset{*}{\Rightarrow} u v^i w x^i y$ for all $i \geq 0$:

$$S \overset{*}{\Rightarrow} uTy \overset{*}{\Rightarrow} uvTxy \overset{*}{\Rightarrow} uvvTxxy \overset{*}{\Rightarrow} \cdots$$

That is, $u v^i w x^i y \in A$ for all $i \geq 0$, which is the main conclusion of the lemma.

To get a bound on the length of vwx, take T to be the lowest variable that is repeated.

The question is: how large must k be? Note that k must work for *all* input. Actually, you have to be a bit more careful. For example, if the grammar contains both $S \to T$ and $T \to S$ as productions, then a string can have an arbitrarily long derivation without working for the lemma (because we forgot to show that vx is not empty).

So, you should start the proof by normalizing the grammar, putting it into Chomsky Normal Form. In this form, every internal node in the derivation tree, except for one directly above a leaf, has two children. It follows that if the tree has more than 2^n leaves, then it has depth more than n. Thus, $k = 2^{n_A} + 1$ will work, where n_A is the number of variables in the Chomsky Normal Form grammar. We leave the details as an exercise. ♦

We will use the notation $z^{(i)}$ to mean the string $u v^i w x^i y$.

Example 9.3
The classic example is $\{\, 0^n 1^n 2^n : n \geq 0 \,\}$. This language is not context-free.

Let k be the constant of the Pumping Lemma. Choose the string $z = 0^k 1^k 2^k$. Consider the split of the string z into $uvwxy$. Because vwx combined has length at most k, the string vx cannot contain both 0's and 2's. This means that $z^{(0)} = uwy$ cannot have equal numbers of 0's, 1's, and 2's (why?), and is therefore not in the language. This is a contradiction.

This is the standard performance. You suppose the language is context-free. Then it must have the properties described by the Pumping Lemma. But you show that it does not have these properties for at least one z. Therefore, it is not context-free.

Example 9.4
Consider the language $\{\, x \# x : x \in \{0,1\}^* \,\}$. (The hash mark is a special symbol that occurs in the middle of the input string.) This language is not context-free.

Let k be the constant of the Pumping Lemma. Choose the string $z = 0^k 1^k \# 0^k 1^k$. Consider the split of the string z into $uvwxy$. Because

$z^{(0)} = uwy$ is in the language, it must still have a # in the middle; so v occurs before the middle of z and x occurs after the middle. But because vwx combined has length at most k, this means that v is a string of 1's and x is a string of 0's, and so $z^{(0)}$ is not in the language after all. This is a contradiction.

Example 9.5   But note that we do not run into a contradiction with $\{\, 0^n 1^n : n \geq 0 \,\}$. For, if we take $z = 0^k 1^k$, then we may write $z = uvwxy$, where the string v is the last 0, the string x is the first 1, and w is empty. With such a choice, $z^{(i)} = uv^i wx^i y$ is in the language.

 For You to Do!   **2.** Show that the language $\{\, \mathsf{a}^i \mathsf{b}^j \mathsf{c}^i \mathsf{d}^j : i, j > 0 \,\}$ is not context-free.

EXERCISES

9.1 Convert the grammar of Example 6.9 into Chomsky Normal Form (assuming "*number*" is a terminal).

9.2 Convert the following grammar with start variable S into Chomsky Normal Form:

$$S \to A S \mathsf{a} \mid \mathsf{a} B$$
$$A \to B \mid S$$
$$B \to \mathsf{b} \mid \varepsilon$$

9.3 Let A be an alphabet and consider any function f that maps symbols in A to nonempty strings in A. Then, for any string w, the string $f(w)$ is defined by replacing each symbol by its f-value. For example, if $A = \{0, 1\}$ and $f(0) = 00$ and $f(1) = 11$, then $f(001) = 000011$. Then, for any language L, the language L^f is defined by $L^f = \{f(w) : w \in L\}$. (The function f is sometimes called a homomorphism.)

    a) Show that if L is context-free, then so is L^f.

    b) Show by example that L^f can be context-free even if L is not.

★ **9.4** Show that the language $\{\mathsf{a}^n \mathsf{b}^{2n} \mathsf{a}^n\}$ is not context-free.

9.5 Show that the language $\{\,0^a1^b2^c \text{ with } a < b < c\,\}$ is not context-free.

9.6 Show that the language $\{\,xx : x \in \{0,1\}^*\,\}$ is not context-free.

Ⓗ **9.7** Show that the complement of the language in the previous question is context-free.

⋆ **9.8** Show that the complement of $\{0^n1^n2^n\}$ is context-free.

9.9 What do the previous two exercises tell us about closure of the set of context-free languages under complements?

9.10 Consider the set of all strings with the unary alphabet $\{\#\}$ with length a perfect square. Show that this language is not context-free.

9.11 Consider the set of all strings with the unary alphabet $\{\#\}$ with length a prime number. Show that this language is not context-free.

⋆ **9.12** Show by example that context-free languages are *not* closed under intersection. Hint: Start with the context-free language $\{\,0^n1^n2^m\,\}$.

9.13 Show that the intersection of a regular language and a context-free language is context-free.

Ⓗ **9.14** Show that a context-free language over a unary alphabet is regular.

9.15 **a)** Give an example of a non-context-free language L such that L^* is not context-free.

   b) Give an example of a non-context-free language M such that M^* is context-free.

⋆ **9.16** Consider the set of all strings of the form x/y, where x and y are positive decimal integers such that $x < y$. The set of such strings represents the set of all possible decimal fractions. Determine if this is a context-free language.

9.17 A CFG is called linear if the right-hand side of every production contains at most one variable. Thus, a regular grammar is always linear. But a linear grammar need not generate a regular language; for example, we saw that palindromes are generated by a linear grammar.

Show that the set of languages generated by linear grammars is closed under union.

Ⓗ **9.18** (Continuation of previous question.) Prove the following Pumping Lemma for linear grammars. If language A has a linear grammar, then there is a constant number k such that for every string $z \in A$ of length at least k, you can split z as $uvwxy$, where: vx is nonempty, $|uvxy| \leq k$, and for all i, $uv^iwx^iy \in A$.

9.19 (Continuation of previous question.) Consider the language $\{\,0^i1^i0^j1^j : i,j > 0\,\}$.

   a) Show that this language is context-free.

   b) Show that this language does not have a linear grammar.

★ **9.20** A context-free grammar is in **Greibach Normal Form** if every production
has a right-hand side that starts with a terminal and the rest is variables.
That is, productions have the form $S \to aB^*$.

Convert the following grammar into Greibach Normal Form:

$$S \to C\,S\,b \mid aa$$
$$C \to ab\,S$$

9.21 A **counter automaton** is an FA that has access to a counter. Equivalently,
it is a PDA that can only push one particular symbol onto the stack.

a) Show that the languages accepted by a deterministic counter automaton are closed under complementation.

b) Show that the languages accepted by a nondeterministic counter automaton are closed under union.

"For You to Do" Exercise Solutions

1. After the first step, you have the following:

$$S \to Ab\,A \mid b\,A \mid Ab \mid b$$
$$A \to Aa \mid a$$

The second step does not apply. After the third step, you have the
following:

$$S \to TA \mid bA \mid Ab \mid b$$
$$A \to Aa \mid a$$
$$T \to Ab$$

And finally, you have the following:

$$S \to TA \mid BA \mid AB \mid b$$
$$A \to AC \mid a$$
$$T \to AB$$
$$B \to b$$
$$C \to a$$

2. Suppose the language is context-free. Let k be the constant of the
Pumping Lemma. Choose the string $z = a^k b^k c^k d^k$. Consider the split
of the string z into $uvwxy$. Because vx is nonempty, it contains some
symbols. However, because vwx combined has length at most k, the
string vx cannot contain both a's and c's, nor can it contain both b's
and d's. Thus, $z^{(0)}$ is not in the language. This is a contradiction.

chapter

10

Deterministic Parsing

The whole idea of grammars and derivation trees is pointless unless there is an efficient procedure for a given grammar to take the string and find a derivation. **Parsing** means getting from the string to the derivation tree and rejecting those strings that are not generated by the grammar. In this chapter, we describe a common algorithm for parsing in a compiler. We also describe a theoretical result that there is a reasonable parsing algorithm for any context-free language.

10.1 Compilers

A compiler for a language such as Java or C starts by building a derivation tree for the input program. The derivation tree reveals the structure of the input. This phase is the task of the **parser**: it essentially determines if and how the input can be derived from the start variable within the rules of the grammar.

There are two competing approaches to parsing. The easiest approach to parsing is top-down parsing. With this, you look at the first symbol of the input to determine which production was used first. If you are lucky, then only one production starts with that symbol, but in general that is not the case. Our conversion from grammar to PDA took a top-down approach, but it had nondeterminism to help it choose. In this book, however, we examine only bottom-up parsing. In this, you start with the input string and try to work backward to the start variable S.

Note that a context-free grammar is not quite sufficient to handle the syntax of a full programming language. The parts that are not describable by such a mechanism are usually easily handled. Such context dependence occurs in rules of type checking or of repeats. For example, many languages have the rule that an identifier cannot be declared twice in the same block. This prohibition cannot be enforced by a context-free grammar. A common strategy is to construct a CFG that is slightly more permissive, accepting a larger language, and then to filter out illicit constructs. On the other hand, accurately describing a language's semantics (meaning) is more difficult.

10.2 Bottom-Up Parsing

Bottom-up parsing is also called **shift–reduce** parsing. Here you read symbols until you have a group that fully matches the right-hand side of a production. Then, you replace that with the left-hand side of the production—called a reduction. And then you continue. This produces a rightmost derivation.

The main question is: should you reduce now, or read the next symbol? We will see that if the CFG is in a certain form, you can tell whether to perform a reduction or to wait until you have more symbols and then perform a different reduction.

The parsing process consists of consecutive steps. There are two kinds of steps:

- **Shift** the next input terminal onto the stack.
- **Reduce** a stacked sequence of symbols to a single variable according to a production. That is, if the subsequence of symbols on top of the stack is the right-hand side of a production, then replace it by the corresponding variable.

The process terminates when you have only the start variable left.

Example 10.1   Recall the grammar for arithmetic expressions (see Example 6.9). Slightly modified, it is as follows:

$$E \to E + T \mid T$$
$$T \to T \times F \mid F$$
$$F \to (E) \mid \mathrm{n}$$

The parsing of $(\mathrm{n} + \mathrm{n}) \times \mathrm{n}$ is given. Note that this parsing *assumes* that the parser knows what to do at each step.

Type	Stack	To be read	Comment
		(n+n)*n	
s	(	n+n)*n	
s	(n	+n)*n	
R	(F	+n)*n	
R	(T	+n)*n	
R	(E	+n)*n	
s	(E+	n)*n	
s	(E+n	)*n	
R	(E+F	)*n	
R	(E+T	)*n	
R	(E	)*n	not reduction T to E
s	(E)	*n	
R	F	*n	
R	T	*n	
s	T*	n	not reduction T to E
s	T*n		
R	T*F		
R	T		not reduction F to T
R	E		

The concrete problem you face in bottom-up parsing is in determining which kind of step to take next and, in the case of a reduce step, which production to use. This question is not easily answered.

It is clear that a nondeterministic PDA can implement a bottom-up parser for any grammar: at each stage it makes the correct choice between shift and reduce, and if reduce, then the correct choice of production. Unfortunately, you cannot always get rid of the nondeterminism. And we most certainly have only deterministic programs. Knuth determined which languages can be recognized by deterministic PDAs. They are given by what are called LR grammars. So, we have to restrict the types of grammars.

10.3 Table-Driven Parser for LR(1) Grammars

An **LR(1) grammar** is defined as a CFG where looking one symbol ahead is enough to decide whether to shift or to reduce.

For efficient parsing, the information on which the decision is to be made must be presented in an appropriate fashion. In the LR(1) parser, this information is given in a **table**. The table tells you if the next operation should be a reduce or a shift. It also has information about the next state of the parser.

In particular, the parser PDA has a current state and a stack. Apart from having terminals on it, the stack is also used to keep track of the state: the entries on the stack alternate between states and symbols (terminal or variable). For example, the stack might be as follows:

$$
\begin{array}{|c|}
\hline
B \\
7 \\
\mathtt{x} \\
4 \\
\vdots \\
\hline
\end{array}
$$

We will number the states.

For each state and each possible next input symbol, the table specifies one of four possible actions:

- *Shift.* (1) Push the current state onto the stack. (2) Read the next symbol and push it onto the stack. (3) Change to the state specified in the table.

  For example: the table entry "s4" means shift and change to state 4.
- *Reduce by the specified production.* (1) Pop the symbols and the intervening states off the stack and discard. (2) Update the state as follows. Say you have reduced to variable X. Look at, but do not pop, the state on top of the stack: say it is q. Then look up in the table what the new state is based on q and X. (3) Push X.

  For example: the entry "R1" means use production 1. Say this is $C \to \mathtt{x}B$ and the stack is as in the preceding picture. Then the reduction pops the B, the state symbol 7 and the $\mathtt{x}$, and discards the three. Now it notes the stack top is 4, pushes the C, and updates its state to that given in row 4 column C.
- *Error.* A blank entry in the table indicates an error in the input.
- *Halt.* And accept.

Example 10.2   Consider the simplified grammar for variable declarations (from Hunter):

1. $S \to \mathtt{real}\ IDLIST$
2. $IDLIST \to IDLIST\,, ID$
3. $IDLIST \to ID$
4. $ID \to \mathtt{A} \mid \mathtt{B} \mid \mathtt{C} \mid \mathtt{D}$

To make it easier to follow, we abbreviate. (In a real parser, the input will already have been converted into such tokens.)

1. $S \rightarrow rL$
2. $L \rightarrow L, I$
3. $L \rightarrow I$
4. $I \rightarrow v$

Each state of the parser corresponds to partial right-hand sides of some productions. This is discussed in more detail later; in this table, we summarize this as "progress". Table 10.1 is the LR(1) table (where eos stands for end-of-string).

State	Progress	r	,	v	eos	S	I	L
0		s1				2		
1	r			s3			4	5
2	S				acc			
3	v		R4		R4			
4	I		R3		R3			
5	rL		s6		R1			
6	L,			s3			7	
7	L, I		R2		R2			

Table 10.1

On input `real A,B`—which we abbreviate `rv,v`—the parser proceeds as follows:

Curr state	Stack	To be read	Operation to apply
0		rv,v	s1
1	0 r	v,v	s3
3	0 r 1 v	,v	R4
4	0 r 1 I	,v	R3
5	0 r 1 L	,v	s6
6	0 r 1 L 5 ,	v	s3
3	0 r 1 L 5 , 6 v		R4
7	0 r 1 L 5 , 6 I		R2
5	0 r 1 L		R1
2	0 S		acc

| Example 10.3 | Recall the grammar from Example 10.1. Let us number the productions: |

1. $E \rightarrow E + T$
2. $E \rightarrow T$
3. $T \rightarrow T \times F$
4. $T \rightarrow F$
5. $F \rightarrow (E)$
6. $F \rightarrow \text{n}$

The table (based on Parsons):

State	Progress	+	×	(	)	n	eos	E	T	F
0				s1		s2		3	4	5
1	(			s1		s2		6	4	5
2	n	R6	R6		R6		R6			
3	E	s7					acc			
4	T	R2	s8		R2		R2			
5	F	R4	R4		R4		R4			
6	(E	s7			s9					
7	E +			s1		s2			10	5
8	T ×			s1		s2				11
9	(E)	R5	R5		R5		R5			
10	E + T	R1	s8		R1		R1			
11	T × F	R3	R3		R3		R3			

Table 10.2

You should at least check that some of the reductions and shifts make sense. For example, if in state 7 an n is read, then it is shifted (so that n is pushed onto the stack) and the progress becomes just the n.

10.4 Construction of an SLR(1) Table

We now describe how to build the table. Technically, this process assumes the grammar is an SLR(1) grammar (S for simple). This process has two main phases: (1) determining the states and the shifts, and (2) determining the reductions. But we start by explaining what each state corresponds to. We use the arithmetic grammar as an example.

10.4.1 Defining the States

The key construct is called an **LR(0)-item**, but we will just call it an **item**. Each item is a production with a certain point on the right-hand side marked—a dot acts as the **marker** and the whole item is enclosed in square brackets. For example $[E \to E + \ \cdot\ T]$ is the production $E \to E + T$ with a marker before the T.

If a production has a right-hand side of length n, then there are $n + 1$ items corresponding to that production. For example, if $S \to \varepsilon$, then there is one item, which is written $[S \to \ \cdot]$. An **initial** item is one where the marker is at the left end; a **completed** item is one where the marker is at the right end.

The intended meaning of an item is that the symbols to the left of the marker have already been read, or reduced to, and they are the top of the stack. It turns out that these items can form the states of a nondeterministic machine. But we need the deterministic version, so we shall go straight there. For our parser,

*each state is a set of items, called an **item-set**.*

It is to be noted that, if the construction goes wrong at any point, that is proof that the grammar is not in the right form. In this book, we deal only with grammars that are of the right form.

The main operation is to determine the item that comes after a given item. This corresponds to a shift from earlier.

1. *Advance the marker.* So, if the item is $[E \to \ \cdot\ (E)]$ and the next symbol is (, go to the item $[E \to (\ \cdot\ E)]$.
2. *Take the closure.* For an item, the **closure** is the set of items as follows: if the marker precedes a variable, then the closure adds all initial items starting with that variable. If one of the new items has a marker preceding a variable, then add all initial items with that variable. And repeat. If the marker precedes a nonterminal, there is nothing to add.

Example 10.4   For the arithmetic grammar, consider the item $[T \to T \ \cdot \times F]$. On the symbol $\times$, the resulting item is $[T \to T \times \ \cdot\ F]$. The closure adds all initial items beginning with F: that is, $[F \to \ \cdot\ (E)]$ and $[F \to \ \cdot n]$.

In general, to find the transition from an item-set rather than a single item, do this process with each item and take the union of the resultant closures.

Determining the next item-set	Let Q be an item-set and σ a symbol. The next item-set is constructed by the following: For each item in Q where the marker precedes σ: **1.** Add the item that results from advancing the marker past σ. **2.** Add the closure of the resultant item.

For the parser to recognize when it is finished, it is standard practice to add a new start variable with its only production taking it to the old start variable. If ever you reduce to the new start variable, you are done. So, in the example, add production 0, which is $E' \to E$. The start item-set is the initial item for the start variable and the closure of this item.

Example 10.5   The start item is $[E' \to \cdot E]$. Its closure adds all initial items starting with E, which in turns adds all initial items starting with T, which in turn adds all initial items starting with F. The start item-set is therefore $\{\,[E' \to \cdot E]$, $[E \to \cdot E + T]$, $[E \to \cdot T]$, $[T \to \cdot T \times F]$, $[T \to \cdot F]$, $[F \to \cdot (E)]$, $[F \to \cdot \mathrm{n}]\,\}$.

10.4.2 Determining the States and Shifts in the Table

We now determine the states and the shifts. Start with the start item-set. Consider every possible next symbol: terminal and variable. For each symbol, determine the next item-set. Then, for each item-set so created, do the same thing. (This process should remind you of the conversion from an NFA with ε-transitions to a DFA.) Repeat until no new item-set is created.

State number	When first occurs (state, symbol)	Items found by moving marker	Initial items added by closure
0	start	$[E' \to \cdot E]$	E, T, F
1	0, (	$[F \to (\cdot E)]$	E, T, F
2	0, n	$[F \to \mathrm{n} \cdot]$	
3	0, E	$[E' \to E \cdot], [E \to E \cdot + T]$	
4	0, T	$[E \to T \cdot], [T \to T \cdot \times F]$	
5	0, F	$[T \to F \cdot]$	
6	1, E	$[F \to (E \cdot)]$	
7	3, +	$[E \to E + \cdot T]$	T, F
8	4, $\times$	$[T \to T \times \cdot F]$	F
9	6,)	$[F \to (E) \cdot]$	
10	7, T	$[E \to E + T \cdot], [T \to T \cdot \times F]$	
11	8, F	$[T \to T \times F \cdot]$	

(The second column is added just to help understand the algorithm.)

At the same time, you start on the table (Table 10.2) from earlier. Each of these transitions produces a shift given in the earlier table. For example, suppose in state 3 you consider the transition for $+$. This defines a new item-set that produces state 7. A shift s7 is added to the table. Note too that some states recur; for example, for state 7 on symbol n, you go back to state 2.

10.4.3 Determining the Reductions

Armed with the states and the shifts, the second phase is to determine the reductions. At one level, the reductions are obvious. Take each completed item and make that a reduction. The issue is that the fundamental question you are trying to answer is *when to reduce and when not to*. And how to recognize an error in the input.

We need the concept of FOLLOW sets. For a variable A, FOLLOW(A) is a set of terminals; specifically, it is the set of all possible terminal symbols that can follow A in a string derived from S. (To be strictly accurate, this definition is only correct if every variable yields at least one string, but that's always the case here.) You include the eos symbol Δ in FOLLOW(A) if the variable A can occur at the end of a derived string. For example, if $S \overset{*}{\Longrightarrow} BCxBAyxC$, then you add y to FOLLOW(A) and Δ, x to FOLLOW(C).

Example 10.6 In the arithmetic grammar, FOLLOW(E) is $\{), \Delta, +\}$. Both FOLLOW(T) and FOLLOW(F) are $\{), \Delta, +, \times\}$. You should verify this. For instance, $E' \overset{*}{\Longrightarrow} E \overset{*}{\Longrightarrow} T \overset{*}{\Longrightarrow} T \times F \overset{*}{\Longrightarrow} F \times F$ shows that $\times \in$ FOLLOW(F).

You can now add the reductions. Specifically:

> *For each completed item, say an A-item, add a reduction to the table for all symbols that occur in* FOLLOW(A). *Except that the reduction corresponding to the artificial production* $E' \to E$ *becomes the acceptance point.*

You can then check that the reductions in Table 10.2 are correct. Note that in no case did a reduction occur where there was already a shift.

This process sounds rather daunting. Fortunately, there is software to do it. The UNIX utility YACC generates LR tables for certain CFGs. For more information, consult the ultimate book by Aho, Sethi, and Ullman, or play around with JFLAP (see page 50).

1. For the grammar of Example 10.2:

   a) Verify that $\text{FOLLOW}(S) = \{\Delta\}$ and $\text{FOLLOW}(L) = \text{FOLLOW}(I) = \{,, \Delta\}$.
   b) Determine the item-sets.
   c) Verify the entries in Table 10.1.

10.5 Guaranteed Parsing

In this section, the goal is an algorithm for any context-free language that determines whether an input string is in the language. This result is mostly of theoretical interest, because the resultant parser is too slow for most practical situations.

The algorithm is called the CYK algorithm, named after Cocke, Younger, and Kasami. It uses a technique known as **dynamic programming**. Dynamic programming is similar to recursion, but it works bottom-up.

The algorithm assumes the context-free language is given by a CFG G in Chomsky Normal Form. If not, the preliminary preprocessing step is to convert the grammar to this form.

Consider an input string w of length n that you want to test whether G generates it. The key idea is to solve a more general problem: you look at substrings of w. Say $w = w_1 w_2 \ldots w_n$. Then, for $1 \le i \le j \le n$, let $w_{i,j}$ be the substring $w_i w_{i+1} \ldots w_j$. The problem you solve is as follows:

which variables produce which substrings.

The point is that suppose $n \ge 2$ and the start variable S produces w. Because G is in Chomsky Normal Form, the first step in the derivation of w must be a production that replaces S by two variables: say $S \to AB$. Then, it follows that the string w can be split into two pieces: the first piece generated from A and the second generated from B. So, the algorithm to determine whether $S \overset{*}{\Longrightarrow} w$ is to determine whether there is a split k and a production $S \to AB$ such that $A \overset{*}{\Longrightarrow} w_{1,k} = w_1 w_2 \ldots w_k$ and $B \overset{*}{\Longrightarrow} w_{k+1,n} = w_{k+1} w_{k+2} \ldots w_n$.

But how to determine whether $A \overset{*}{\Longrightarrow} w_{1,k}$? Thinking recursively, we see that the same idea continues. In general, suppose you want to know if variable $A \overset{*}{\Longrightarrow} w_{i,j}$ for some i and j. Consider all possible productions from A. For each such production, say $A \to EF$, try all possible k from i up to $j - 1$. For each k, ask whether $E \overset{*}{\Longrightarrow} w_{i,k}$ and $F \overset{*}{\Longrightarrow} w_{k+1,j}$.

To make this efficient, you work from the bottom up; that is, answer the question for smaller strings first. A table is used to keep track of the answers so far.

CYK algorithm

1. Start by answering for each i and each variable A whether $A \overset{*}{\Longrightarrow} w_{i,i}$. In this case, the substring $w_{i,i}$ is just a single symbol; so you simply look at the unit productions of G.
2. Then answer for each i and each variable A whether $A \overset{*}{\Longrightarrow} w_{i,i+1}$. In this case, you use the general recipe provided earlier.
3. Repeat for all $w_{i,i+2}$, then for all $w_{i,i+3}$, and so on. At each stage, determine completely the set of variables that produces the substrings of that length, and then increase the length.

At the final stage, you determine the variables for substrings of length n. Well, actually $w = w_{1,n}$ itself is the only such substring. This enables you to answer the original question: whether $S \overset{*}{\Longrightarrow} w$ or not.

Example 10.7

Consider the CFG with start variable S:

$$S \to ST \mid TU \mid \mathtt{b}$$
$$T \to SU \mid \mathtt{a}$$
$$U \to SS \mid \mathtt{b}$$

Consider the input string $w = \mathtt{aababb}$.
The table constructed is as follows:

		1	2	3	4	5	6
	1	T	.	.	.	S	S,T,U
	2		T	S	S	S,T,U	S,T,U
start	3			S,U	S	T,U	S,T,U
	4				T	S	S,T,U
	5					S,U	T,U
	6						S,U

finish

What does this table mean? Consider for example the entry in row 3 column 5. This entry says that variables T and U generate the string $w_{3,5}$ (which is $\mathtt{bab}$). This entry was calculated by the algorithm. For example, the variable T is here because $T \to SU$ (one of the productions) and $S \overset{*}{\Longrightarrow} w_{3,4}$, $U \overset{*}{\Longrightarrow} w_{5,5}$ (look to the left of and down from this entry).

Because S is in the entry in row 1 column 6, it follows that w is in the language. With a bit more effort you can read off a derivation from the table. This entails recording (or recalculating) where the entries came from. For example, the S is there since $T \overset{*}{\Longrightarrow} w_{1,1}$ and $U \overset{*}{\Longrightarrow} w_{2,6}$. The U in the entry for $w_{2,6}$ is there for two splits, including $S \overset{*}{\Longrightarrow} w_{2,3}$ and $S \overset{*}{\Longrightarrow} w_{4,6}$. And so on.

For You to Do!

2. For the abbreviated grammar of Example 10.2, convert to Chomsky Normal Form, and then apply the CYK algorithm to the string `rv,v,v`.

EXERCISES

10.1 Consider the CFG

1. $S \to \text{aa}S$
2. $S \to \text{b}$

The SLR(1) table is

State	a	b	eos	S
0	s1	s2		3
1	s4			
2			R2	
3			*acc*	
4	s1	s2		5
5			R1	

a) Show the steps in parsing aaaab.
b) Show the steps in parsing aaabab (which is not in the language).
c) Determine the item-sets.
d) Determine FOLLOW(S).

10.2 Consider the CFG with start variable S:

1. $S \to AX$
2. $A \to \text{a}$
3. $A \to \text{b}$
4. $X \to \text{x}$
5. $X \to \text{y}$

Derive the item-sets and the table for an LR-parser for this grammar.

10.3 Consider the CFG with start variable S:

    1. $S \to E$
    2. $E \to E + T$
    3. $E \to T$
    4. $T \to \mathrm{n}$

    Derive the item-sets and the table for an LR-parser for this grammar.

★ **10.4** Consider the CFG (think M as method and P as parameter):

    1. $M \to \mathrm{v}(P)$
    2. $P \to P, \mathrm{v} \mid \mathrm{v}$

    a) Derive the item-sets and the table for an LR-parser for this grammar.
    b) Then show how the string $\mathrm{v(v,v)}$ is parsed.

10.5 Consider the CFG with start variable T:

    1. $T \to B \mid \{L\}$
    2. $L \to TL \mid B$
    3. $B \to \mathrm{a} \mid \mathrm{b}$

    Derive the item-sets and the table for an LR-parser for this grammar.

10.6 Consider the CFG (think of i as "if" and e as "else"):

$$S \to \mathrm{i}Se S \mid \mathrm{i}S \mid \mathrm{a}$$

    a) Compute FOLLOW(S).
    b) Compute the item-sets for this grammar.
    c) Attempt to compute the SLR(1) table. There should be in one position a conflict between a reduce and a shift.
    d) Show that the string iiaea has two derivation trees.
    e) Discuss the connection between your answer in Part (d) and the conflict found in Part (c).
    f) In computer languages, the construct if ... if ... else ... is called the "dangling else" problem, because it is not immediately clear which if the else applies to. The standard solution is to define that the else applies to the most recent if. Use this to resolve the conflict in the table.

10.7 Consider the CFG for $\{\, 0^n 1^n : n > 0 \,\}$:

$$S \to 0S1 \mid 01$$

    Convert to Chomsky Normal Form and then apply the CYK algorithm to the string 000111.

★ **10.8** Consider the Chomsky Normal Form grammar from Example 9.1. Apply the CYK algorithm to the string `aababa`.

10.9 In your favorite programming language, code up the CYK algorithm.

10.10 For a variable A, the set FIRST(A) is the set of all possible first terminals in strings derived from A.

    a) Show that FIRST(S) = {r} and FIRST(I) = FIRST(L) = {v} for the grammar of Example 10.2.

    b) Determine the FIRST sets for the grammar of Example 10.1.

10.11 (Continuation of previous question.) Assuming you have calculated the FIRST sets, there is an algorithm for the FOLLOW sets.

> We assume all variables can occur and every one generates at least one string of terminals.
>
> Start with FOLLOW(S) = {Δ} and all other FOLLOW sets empty.
>
> Repeat the following until nothing changes:
>
> - For every production $Q \rightarrow \ldots A y \ldots$, add y to FOLLOW(A).
> - For every production $Q \rightarrow \ldots A B \ldots$, add FIRST($B$) to FOLLOW($A$).
> - For every production $Q \rightarrow \ldots A$, add FOLLOW(Q) to FOLLOW(A).

    a) Write down the algorithm in more detail and provide a justification for it.

    b) Use the algorithm to calculate the FOLLOW sets for the grammars of Examples 10.2 and 10.3.

"For You to Do" Exercise Solutions

1.

State	Contents of item-set
0	$[S' \rightarrow \cdot S], [S \rightarrow \cdot rL]$
1	$[S \rightarrow r \cdot L], [L \rightarrow \cdot L, I], [L \rightarrow \cdot I], [I \rightarrow \cdot v]$
2	$[S' \rightarrow S \cdot]$
3	$[I \rightarrow v \cdot]$
4	$[L \rightarrow I \cdot]$
5	$[S \rightarrow rL \cdot], [L \rightarrow L \cdot, I]$
6	$[L \rightarrow L, \cdot I], [I \rightarrow \cdot v]$
7	$[L \rightarrow L, I \cdot]$

2. One Chomsky Normal Form is

$$S \rightarrow RL \mid RI$$
$$L \rightarrow LF \mid IF$$
$$F \rightarrow CI$$
$$I \rightarrow \text{v}$$
$$C \rightarrow \text{,}$$
$$R \rightarrow \text{r}$$

The resulting table is

	1	2	3	4	5	6
1	R	S	.	S	.	S
2		I	.	L	.	L
3			C	F	.	.
4				I	.	L
5					C	F
6						I

SUMMARY

A context-free grammar (CFG) consists of a set of productions that you can use to replace a variable by a string of variables and terminals. The language of a grammar is the set of strings it generates. A language is context-free if there is a CFG for it. Each string in the language has a leftmost derivation and a derivation tree. If these are unique for all strings, then the grammar is called unambiguous.

A pushdown automaton (PDA) is an FA with a stack added for storage. We choose to draw these as flowcharts where the character Δ indicates both empty stack and end-of-input. A PDA is nondeterministic by definition.

There is an algorithm to convert a CFG to an equivalent PDA: the PDA guesses the leftmost derivation. The algorithm to convert from PDA to CFG is more complex.

A regular grammar is one where every production has the form $A \rightarrow bC$ or $A \rightarrow a$. The Chomsky hierarchy also includes context-sensitive grammars and unrestricted grammars.

There are special forms for CFGs such as Chomsky Normal Form, where every production has the form $A \rightarrow BC$ or $A \rightarrow c$. The algorithm to convert to Chomsky Normal Form involves (1) determining all nullable variables and getting rid of all ε-productions, (2) getting rid of all variable unit productions, (3) breaking up long productions, and (4) moving terminals to unit productions.

Context-free languages are closed under the Kleene operations but not under intersection or complementation. The Pumping Lemma can be used to prove that a language is not context-free.

Parsing can be performed top down or bottom up. In the latter, the string is processed through a series of shifts (pushing input symbol) and reductions (replacing right-hand side of production by left-hand variable). A table can be produced for efficient parsing. The CYK algorithm can be used to parse any context-free language.

*Grammars occur in several areas of artificial intelligence (AI). The most obvious application is in speech recognition and **natural language processing**. However, CFGs by themselves define only syntax and so cannot ensure that the resultant sentence is meaningful—hence Chomsky's quote at the beginning of this part. Language also has pieces that are sort of context-sensitive. For example, the subject, verb, and associated pronouns must agree: "I am riding my bike," "You are riding your bike."*

*For understanding and processing natural language, one common approach is to augment grammars. An example of this is an **augmented transition network grammar**: every arc of the grammar network has actions associated with it that help achieve structure and avoid meaningless parsing. Another approach is to reduce the grammar complexity through the use of variables that have parameters.*

*Another AI application of CFGs is in **grammar induction**. This is a mechanism to discover patterns in data; specifically, it assumes there is an underlying CFG or regular grammar, and tries to learn or induce the grammar from the data. This mechanism has been applied to solve problems in areas such as intelligent agents, data mining, and biochemistry.*

For an in-depth discussion of the possibilities (and limitations), consult the ultimate AI book by Russell and Norvig.

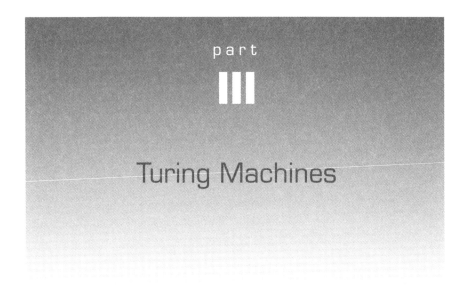

part

III

Turing Machines

We have seen that FAs, REs, PDAs, and CFGs are not powerful enough to handle all languages or all situations. The most powerful model of a computer is the Turing machine. This model was investigated by Turing and Post and others more than 60 years ago, before the invention of computers. In fact, their theoretical results greatly influenced the design of the digital computer.

At first sight, a Turing machine appears primitive: just a finite automaton with a tape. But the ability to arbitrarily write on and access the tape provides considerable leverage. Indeed, we will see that the Turing machine is a model of a real-world computer; and further we will argue that it captures the notion of an "effective computer." Thus, Turing machines have the same abilities and the same inabilities as any computer we have.

One machine can do the work of fifty ordinary men. No machine can do the work of one extraordinary man.
—**Elbert Hubbard**

Machines are worshipped because they are beautiful, and valued because they confer power; they are hated because they are hideous, and loathed because they impose slavery.
—**Bertrand Russell**

The limits of my language are the limits of my world.
—**Ludwig Wittgenstein**

Turing Machines

The most powerful model of a computer is the Turing machine. This is an FA with an infinite tape on which it can write.

11.1 A Turing Machine Has a Tape

What would it take to be a human computer? In particular, what memory would be required? Imagine having a big sheet of paper. What would you do? You might add a symbol. Or erase a symbol. Or move a symbol. This idea is embodied in the notion of a tape: an infinitely long piece of paper divided up into squares.

A **Turing machine** (TM) is a machine like an FA, but it is allowed to write on the tape and to move its head left and right. More precisely, a TM has three components:

- An **infinite tape** divided up into cells. Each **cell** contains one symbol. The symbol Δ denotes the empty or **blank** cell.
- A **head** that can access one cell at a time, and that can both read from and write on the tape, and can move both left and right. The **input** is presented on the tape surrounded by Δ; the head starts at the left-most symbol. (If the input is the empty string, then the tape is empty and the head points to an empty cell.)
- A **memory** that is in one of a fixed finite number of states. Like the PDA, once a TM enters an accept state, it stops.

Here is a TM with input 001:

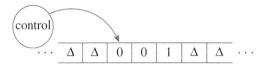

We assume a **two-way infinite** tape: it stretches to infinity in both directions. However, only a finite part of the tape is nonblank at any point.

The **program** of a TM is a transition function; depending on the symbol under the head and the state, the machine takes the following actions:

1. Writes a symbol
2. Moves left or right or stays in place
3. Updates its state

The program is represented as a diagram like that of an FA, except that each arrow is labeled not with a single symbol but with a triple:

$$\text{oldSymbol} \quad \text{newSymbol} \quad \text{moveDir}$$

where the "moveDir" is one of L, which means move left one cell; R, which means move right one cell; and S, which means do not move head (left/right/stay). For example, the triple 01L means "if reading a 0, then write a 1 and move the head left." As in a PDA, the machine can terminate abnormally if there is no transition.

More formally, we can define a TM as a 7-tuple $(Q, \Sigma, \Gamma, q_0, h_a, h_r, \delta)$ where:

- Q is a set of states.
- Σ denotes the input alphabet.
- Γ denotes the tape alphabet: It is useful for the TM to have additional symbols at its disposal that cannot appear in the input. In other words, the **tape alphabet** is a proper superset of the **input alphabet**; for example, it includes the special symbol Δ (the blank).
- q_0 is the start state. The state h_a always denotes the unique accept state, and the state h_r always denotes the unique reject state (which is seldom drawn); if the machine enters either of these states, then it halts immediately.
- δ denotes the transition function $Q \times \Gamma \mapsto Q \times \Gamma \times \{L, R, S\}$. For example, $\delta(q, 0) = (r, 1, S)$ means that in state q on reading a 0, the machine changes to state r, writes a 1, and does not move the head.

The **language** of a TM is the set of all strings such that the TM, when started with the string on its tape, eventually enters the state h_a. If M is the TM, then we use $L(M)$ to denote its language. We also say that the TM is a **recognizer** for its language.

Example 11.1

Here is a TM for the regular language consisting of all binary strings that contain the substring 101. In this case, the TM always writes the symbol that it has just read and always moves right. (But most of the time, the TM program will be more complex.)

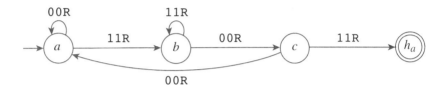

Example 11.2

A TM that accepts $\{\, 0^n 1^n \,\}$. The idea is to pair off the 0's and 1's. More precisely, repeatedly erase the first 0 and the last 1 until the empty string is reached. In pseudocode:

1. If HeadSymbol=0 then Write(Blank) else Reject.
2. Move head right until HeadSymbol=Blank.
3. Move head left.
4. If HeadSymbol=1 then Write(Blank) else Reject.
5. Move head left until HeadSymbol=Blank.
6. Move head right.
7. If HeadSymbol=Blank then Accept.
8. Goto (1).

The TM is drawn in Figure 11.1, together with an illustration of what happens on input 00111, which is rejected.

We will see several variations of a TM later.

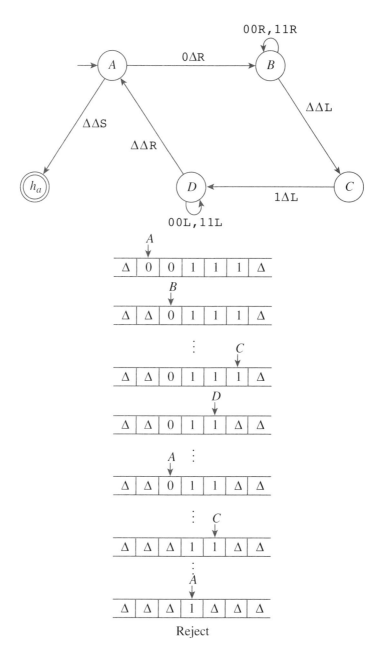

Figure 11.1 A TM for $\{0^n1^n\}$ and its action on 00111

11.2 More Examples

Here is a particularly unhelpful TM. What does it do? It goes back and forth converting a's to b's and back again. This example does introduce an important possibility: a TM might not halt.

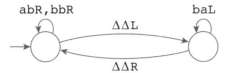

Balanced brackets. (See Example 7.2.)

The idea is to find the innermost matching pair of brackets, then erase them, and repeat the process. We use a special symbol to indicate an erased bracket—the symbol x. (You cannot simply erase a bracket by using a blank because then you would lose track of where the string begins and ends.)

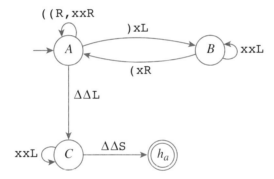

The states of the TM can be interpreted as follows:

A: Search rightward for the first); when found, cross out & goto B; if none found goto C.

B: Search leftward for (to match; when found, cross out & goto A.

C: This state is reached when there are no more); search leftward for leftover (; if none found then Accept else Reject.

For example, this machine rejects ()))(but accepts (()(())).

It is important to remember that the TM is the sum total of the machine and its operating system. So, when you build a TM, you define your own tape alphabet, your own finite-state control, and so forth. But once designed, these elements are fixed.

Example 11.4

Palindromes.

Here is a TM that accepts even-length binary palindromes. The idea is to match the first and last symbols and erase them; then repeat. If you get down to the empty string without a mismatch, then the string was a palindrome. We need six states; call them A, B_0, B_1, C_0, C_1, D.

A: If string empty then accept; else examine & erase leftmost symbol; if a 0 goto B_0 else goto B_1.
B_j: Reached if first symbol was j; goto right end of string; when found goto C_j.
C_j: If last symbol not matches, then reject; else erase symbol & goto D.
D: Rewind string; then goto A.

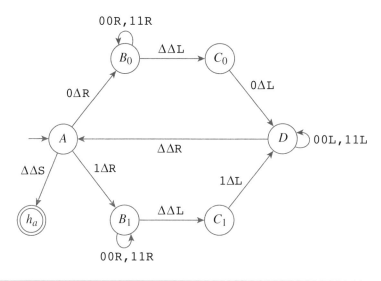

We will often be much more informal and present a TM as pseudocode or as an English description.

Example 11.5

A TM that recognizes $\{\, w\#w : w \in \Sigma^* \,\}$ (this language is not context-free).

The TM crosses off the first entry and remembers it. It then marches off along the string until it gets to the first entry after the hash mark. It checks that that is correct and crosses that off. It returns to the leftmost uncrossed entry and repeats the process, ignoring the crossed-out symbols. The TM accepts if it manages to cross out all the symbols without running into a problem.

11.3 TM Subroutines

What exactly is a TM? At this stage, it looks like a TM is a simple computer perhaps with a limited instruction set. However, we will see that it can perform complex tasks. One aid to this is to design TM subroutines: basic tasks that are useful.

Example 11.6

A TM that shifts the entire input string one cell to the right.

One idea is to move the rightmost symbol over, and then the next one, and so on. The following TM moves to the end of the string, remembering the last symbol seen as it goes. When it reaches the right-hand end, it writes down the remembered symbol, then backs up and erases the symbol. It then backs up one more and shifts that symbol over, and repeats. (It may help to step through this machine by hand.)

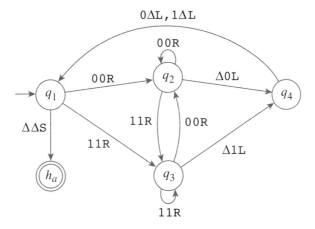

The approach in Example 11.6 is a little inefficient. An exercise in this chapter asks for a TM that does this shift in a single pass over the string.

11.4 TMs That Do Not Halt

Another dimension that we have now in our model of computation is that the machine does not necessarily halt. If the input string is in the language, then the machine must halt (in a finite number of steps) and end in the accept state. But for a string that is not in the language of that machine, the TM can get stuck in a loop. Or even without looping the TM can go on forever.

And, moreover, we might not know beforehand if it will stop. Consider, for example, a TM that tries to find a counterexample to **Goldbach's conjecture**. This unsolved conjecture states that every even number at least 4 is the sum of two primes. The TM tries every even value of n in increasing order. For each n, it checks if there is a value of i such that both i and $n-i$ are prime. If not, it stops. Otherwise, it continues forever. So, we have built a TM for which we humans don't know whether it halts or not.

But there are stranger things to come.

 For You to Do!

1. Draw the diagram for a TM that accepts the language $\{0^n1^n2^n\}$.

EXERCISES

11.1 Consider the following TM. For each of these strings, show the final tape and say whether the TM accepts it or not:

a) 0011
b) 101010
c) 110
d) 00100

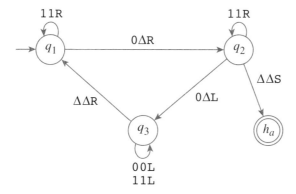

11.2 Adapt the TM of Example 11.4 to accept all binary palindromes.

11.3 Convert the TM that accepts $\{w\#w\}$ in Example 11.5 into a diagram. (Assume the alphabet for w is $\{0, 1\}$.)

★ **11.4** Draw the diagram for a TM that accepts all binary strings of odd length with a 0 in the middle.

11.5 Draw the diagram for a TM that accepts $\{0^a 1^b : a < b\}$.

11.6 Draw the diagram for a TM that accepts $\{w\#w\#w : w \in \{0, 1\}^*\}$.

11.7 Draw the diagram for a TM that accepts $\{a^{2^n} : n > 0\}$.

★ **11.8** Draw the diagram for a TM that accepts all strings $\{wx : |w| = |x|, w \neq x\}$. (Assume the alphabet is $\{0, 1\}$.)

11.9 Draw the diagram for a TM that accepts $\{0^a 1^b 0^c : a + c = b\}$.

11.10 Describe (without the details) a TM that accepts all binary strings with an equal number of 0's and 1's.

11.11 Describe (without the details) a TM that accepts all binary strings with the number of 0's double that of the number of 1's.

★ **11.12** In a string, a **block** is a substring of all the same letters that cannot be extended. For example, 11100001 has three blocks. Give the diagram for a TM that accepts all binary strings such that there is an even number of blocks, every block has the same length, and the string starts with a block of zeroes. For example, 00110011, 00001111, and 01010101 are in the language.

11.13 The following TM has alphabet $\{0, 1\}$.

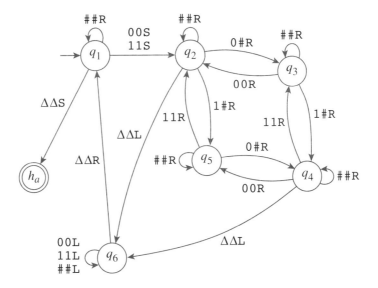

    a) Is the empty string accepted?

    b) The only symbol the TM writes on the tape is #. What does this suggest about the role of that symbol?

    c) If the input is a string of ninety-nine 0's, what is the last state before rejection?

    d) Which four-symbol strings does the TM accept?

    (H) e) What is the language of this TM?

11.14 Consider the following TM with input alphabet $\{0,1\}$.

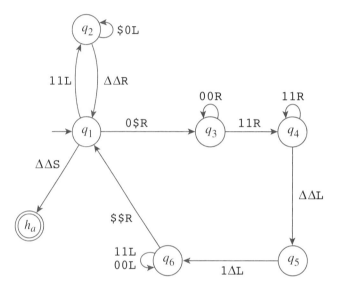

    a) What happens to the TM if the first symbol of the input is a 1?

    b) What is the final string if the input is 0011?

    c) Which four-symbol strings does the TM accept?

    d) What is the language of this TM?

11.15 Draw the diagram for a TM that shifts the entire input string one cell to the right and never moves its head left.

★ 11.16 Describe a TM subroutine that reverses the string on its tape.

11.17 Describe a TM subroutine that effectively deletes a symbol; that is, it deletes the symbol and shifts left all symbols to the right of this point.

11.18 In your favorite programming language, write a TM simulator. The TM should be stored as a file with a standard format.

    For example, the format might be as follows:

        First line is the number of states (numbered from 0).

        Second line is the start state.

Third line is the accept state.

Fourth line is the symbols in the tape alphabet (apart from blank).

The remaining lines in the file are the transitions. Each line is of the form F T RWM, where the transition goes from F to T, and R=readSymbol, W=writeSymbol (where D stands for blank symbol), and M=headMoveChar (L for left, R for right, S for stationary).

"For You to Do" Exercise Solutions

1.

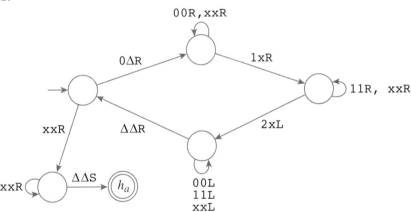

Variations of Turing Machines

The fundamental question is to determine the power of TMs. In this, we do not worry about the speed; only what a TM can and cannot do. In this chapter, we show that changing the model, making it less or more restrictive, usually does not change the power of a TM.

12.1 TMs as Transducers

We have focused on machines that are recognizers for languages. But you can also design machines that perform **calculations**. Such a machine is sometimes called a **transducer**.

In the case of a TM, the calculation is performed by the TM leaving the answer (its output, if you like) on the tape. For example, a TM that starts with $\$^i\#\$^j$ on the tape and ends with $\$^{ij}$ on the tape does multiplication.

Example 12.1

Here is a TM that treats the input as a unary number and divides the input by 2 (that is, it cuts the string's length in half). (The alphabet is $\{0\}$.)

The idea is to change the first symbol to another symbol, and then delete the last symbol. And repeat this process. At the end of the calculation, you could change the new symbol back to the old symbol, but this TM does not; it leaves a string of $'s.

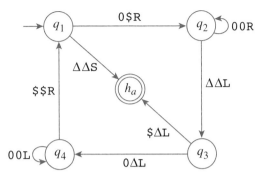

Note that if the input has odd length, the TM rounds down.

A function f, which converts strings into strings, is defined to be **T-computable** if and only if there exists a TM M that computes it. That is, M always halts, and on input w, M halts with the string $f(w)$ on its tape. You can also consider **partial functions**: these are functions that are undefined for some strings; that is, where the TM might not halt for some of the input.

12.2 Variations on the Model

It turns out that the definition of a Turing machine is a very robust concept; giving the machine extra heads or tapes or whatever tends not to alter the power of the machine. There is a parallel with programming languages: Java and Basic might look different, but it is clear that anything that can be programmed in one can be programmed in the other (you can even write a compiler in the one language for the other). We define the original as the **standard TM**.

How do you show that a variation does not alter the machine's power? The general idea in TMs is to show the following:

> *If you add or subtract a feature, then you can adjust the program to cater for this.*

This might entail adding extra states or reorganizing the way the data is stored on the tape. If a capability is added, then you show that the standard TM can simulate that capability; if a capability is removed, then you show that the crippled TM can simulate the standard one.

For example, what happens if we omit the stay-put option? That is, we force the TM to move its head each time. Well, how can we achieve the net effect? The idea is simple: move the head off the cell and immediately move the head back. How do we ensure that the head moves back? Move to a special intermediate state that has been added to the program. For example, a transition $\delta(q, 0) = (r, 1, S)$ becomes $\delta(q, 0) = (x, 1, L)$, and $\delta(x, ANY) = (r, R, ANY)$, where x is a newly introduced state.

What about having several heads? Call a multiheaded TM the **Medusa**. Well, a standard machine could simulate the Medusa by storing on its tape the location of the Medusa's heads. For example, the standard machine could represent each Medusan head by a new symbol $\#_1$, $\#_2$, and so forth. If the Medusa had two heads:

To simulate one step of the Medusa, the standard machine sweeps along the entire length of the string, finds each Medusan head, and updates it. Note that the important thing here is simulation—the number of steps needed might be enormous (it isn't), but that is utterly irrelevant. The question is what a TM can and cannot accept.

12.3 Multiple Tapes

Consider a variation of a TM with multiple tracks. For example, a **two-track TM** is one where there are two symbols in each cell, an upper one and a lower one. The way to simulate this is to create a new alphabet: each letter of the alphabet represents an ordered pair of symbols.

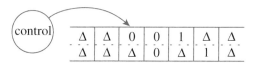

To show that a TM with multiple tapes has the same power as a standard TM is not much harder.

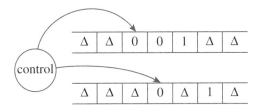

One approach is to convert a multitape TM to a multitrack TM, storing the positions of the heads as in the preceding Medusan example. Another approach is to store all the tapes' contents side by side on a single tape, separated by some special symbol. The argument is left as an exercise.

12.4 Nondeterminism and Halting

One surprise (to me, at least) is that nondeterminism does not add anything to the power of a TM! So, what does nondeterminism entail? It means that at any step the TM may have more than one choice of action. As usual, we define that a nondeterministic TM (or **NTM**) accepts a string if there exists some choice of actions that leads to the accept state.

We need the concept of a **configuration**. A configuration records the complete status of a machine: its state, the contents of the tapes, the position of the heads, and so on.

Theorem	A nondeterministic TM has the same power as a standard TM.

Proof   We must show that the NTM can be simulated by a deterministic one. Well, in a simulation simply try all possible choices!

We can represent the calculations of the nondeterministic machine NTM as a tree branching out forever. The nodes of the tree represent the possible *configurations* of the NTM, and the children of a node are the possible next steps of the machine. The NTM accepts the input if and only if there is a finite branch that leads to an accepting configuration.

Now, the simulator must not go on down one branch exclusively, because that branch might lead on forever. Instead, it does a breadth-first search. For this, it keeps a large **queue** of nodes whose children it has not considered. Of course, the running time explodes. But that is not the point. If one of the branches reaches an accept state and halts, then our simulator, tortoise that it is, will reach there eventually.

♦

Unless otherwise stated, we assume that our TMs are deterministic because this makes proving facts about the languages accepted by a TM a bit easier.

12.5 Church's Thesis

At first glance, a TM appears to be a rather primitive device. Being able to access the tape only sequentially seems a problem. But it is not too hard to show that if you are given a second tape to store the address of a cell on the first tape, you can use the first tape as **random access memory**, as in a normal computer. With a few more ideas, you can even do without the extra tape. And pretty soon you can show that you can translate any program for a normal computer into a program for a TM.

Fact	A Turing machine can simulate a real computer.

Several models of computation have been proposed over the years. They all turn out to have exactly the same power as a TM as recognizers; the definition of a TM is a very robust concept.

Turing introduced his model of a computer in about 1936 in the midst of work by several people on what computation means and what can be computed. Prominent among these were Gödel, Church, and Post. What has become known as Church's "thesis" (in the sense of a belief or tenet) is that the model is appropriate and has all the power of *any* computer we might build.

Church's thesis	There is an "effective procedure" for a problem if and only if there is a TM for the problem.

Nowadays we use the word *algorithm* instead of *effective procedure*.

12.6 Universal TMs

Indeed, one interesting question is whether one TM can simulate another TM. A **universal TM** is a TM that takes another TM as an input. For this, you need to specify an **encoding** of a TM; a series of triples will do for the transition function. The simplest idea for a universal TM is to have three tapes: the first holds the input, the second is the working tape (initialized from the input tape), and the third remembers the state of the TM being simulated. Universal TMs have been devised with surprisingly few states.

For You to Do!

1. Draw a TM that erases all instances of a certain symbol from the input. To be specific, let's say the alphabet is $\{0,1\}$ and the TM erases all 1's. For example, if the input is 10101100, then the output is 0000.
2. A Jittery TM is one that always writes a symbol different from the one it has just read. Show that a Jittery TM can simulate a standard TM.

EXERCISES

12.1 For unary input, draw a TM that computes the parity. That is, it leaves one symbol if the input length is odd, and zero symbols otherwise.

12.2 Draw a TM with alphabet $\{a,b\}$ that for any input changes all a's to b's and vice versa.

12.3 Write TMs that treat the input as a unary number and do the following:

a) Double the input
b) Triple the input
c) Compute the remainder when the input is divided by 3

★ **12.4** Write TMs that have as input two unary numbers separated by a special symbol $ and

a) determine which is the smaller number (accept if first smaller)
b) determine if the two numbers are equal (accept if equal)

12.5 Draw a TM for concatenation. That is, it starts with two strings x and y separated by a special symbol $ and ends with the string xy.

12.6 Draw a TM to compute the string function $f(x) = x\$x^R$. That is, it appends a copy of the string, except that the second copy is reversed, with the first and second copies separated by a special symbol. For example, if it starts with 0100 on tape, the TM should end with 0100$0010.

12.7 Write out in detail the proof that a two-tape TM is no more powerful than a one-tape TM.

★ **12.8** Describe a two-tape machine that does the following:

a) With a unary number on the first tape, constructs the binary equivalent on the second tape.
b) With a binary number on the second tape, constructs the unary equivalent on the first tape.

12.9 Show that if a TM has two tapes, and a binary number is written on the first tape, then you can advance the second head by that amount.

12.10 Describe a TM that has as input two binary numbers separated by $ and computes the minimum of the two numbers.

(H) **12.11** Draw a TM for the addition of two binary numbers.

★ **12.12** The **hailstones** problem is the following: on input of an integer, repeat the following. If the number is odd, multiply by 3 and add 1. If the number is even, divide by 2. Repeat until the number becomes 1. For example, starting with 3, the sequence is 3, 10, 5, 16, 8, 4, 2, 1. (It is believed, but not known, that the process halts for all integers.)

a) Draw a TM that multiplies a number in binary by 3.
b) Give a rough description of a TM that performs the hailstones problem.

12.13 Consider the following TM.

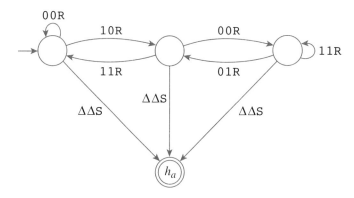

a) If the input string is 10101, what is the final configuration of the TM?
b) Does this TM halt on all strings?
c) What exactly does this TM do to the string on the input tape? (Hint: Consider the string as a binary number.)

12.14 The following TM is nondeterministic:

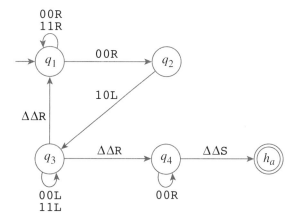

a) The string 01 is accepted. Show the final configuration for one accepting computation.

b) Give a string of length 3 that is **not** accepted.

c) Determine the language of this machine.

12.15 Suppose you have a TM M for language L. Describe in English how to build a nondeterministic TM for language L^*.

★ **12.16** Describe a nondeterministic two-tape TM for testing whether the string on the first tape is a substring of the string on the second tape.

Ⓗ **12.17** Consider a TM that is not allowed to change state and move head simultaneously. Show that this version has the same power as a standard TM.

12.18 Consider a TM that is not allowed to write a blank on a cell that is not blank. Show that this version has the same power as a standard TM.

12.19 Sometimes a TM is defined to have a **one-way infinite tape** (that is, a tape that has a start but no end). The input is written at the start of the tape. The machine crashes if it tries to move off the left end of the tape.

Sketch how to convert a program that runs on the standard TM model to that model, and vice versa. (It may help to think of a special symbol being present at the start of the one-way infinite tape.)

★ **12.20** (See previous question.) Consider a one-way infinite TM that, when it moves left, automatically moves to the leftmost cell; call this a Left-Reset TM. Show that a Left-Reset TM can simulate a standard TM.

Ⓗ **12.21** A counter automaton was introduced in Exercise 9.21. Show that a deterministic counter automaton cannot recognize the language $\{w\#w^R\}$ (palindromes where the middle is indicated).

Ⓗ **12.22** A multicounter automaton is a machine having a fixed number of counters. The only operations that can be applied to a counter are to increment it, decrement it, and test for zero. Show that a multicounter automaton with a sufficient number of counters can simulate the behavior of a standard TM.

12.23 Construct a TM that halts if and only if the tape contains a nonempty cell. In this question, the head can start anywhere on the tape.

★ **12.24** Recall from Exercise 8.11 that a **2-PDA** is like a PDA except that it has two stacks. Show that a TM can simulate a 2-PDA.

Ⓗ **12.25** A **queue automaton** is like a PDA except that it has a queue instead of a stack. (A queue is first-in, first-out.) That is, it is a DFA together with a queue of symbols such that it can examine and remove from the front of the queue and add to the back of the queue. Show that a queue automaton can simulate a standard TM.

12.26 (TERM PAPER) "Models of computation are essential to the study of computer science but are of little practical use." Discuss with specific reference to finite automata, grammars, and Turing machines.

12.27 Convince your life partner that a TM can do anything a PDA can.

"For You to Do" Exercise Solutions

1. The idea is to move each 0 to the left; then erase the 1's.

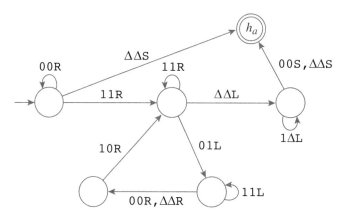

2. For each symbol in the tape alphabet, add a copy of that symbol to the tape alphabet. Then, for each move of the standard TM, the Jittery TM makes two moves: it first writes the duplicate symbol, staying put but going to a temporary state; then it writes the real symbol and moves to the correct state. For example, the transition $\delta(q,0) = (r,0,L)$ becomes $\delta(q,0) = (q',0',S)$ and $\delta(q',0') = (r,0,L)$.

chapter

13

Decidable Problems and Recursive Languages

The recursive languages are those that can be recognized by TMs that always halt. We examine these here. They are related to questions whose answers can be computed.

13.1 Recursive and Recursively Enumerable Languages

A language is **recursively enumerable** (r.e.) if it is the set of strings accepted by some TM. A language is **recursive** if it is the set of strings accepted by some TM that halts on *every* input. For example, any regular language is recursive. It will take a while, but we will eventually show that there are many languages that are r.e. but not recursive, and that there are many languages that are not even r.e.

We start with some properties of these sets of languages.

Fact
 a) The set of r.e. languages is closed under union and intersection.
 b) The set of recursive languages is closed under union and intersection.

Proof
 Proof of (a) Say the languages L_1 and L_2 are r.e., being accepted by machines M_1 and M_2. A machine for $L_1 \cup L_2$ simply runs the two machines M_1 and M_2 in *parallel*—the input string is in the union exactly when at

least one machine halts and accepts. A similar idea works for $L_1 \cap L_2$. The string is in the intersection exactly when both machines halt and accept.

The proof of Part (b) is left as an exercise.

♦

Note that in (a) you need to run M_1 and M_2 in parallel: you cannot run M_1 (say) first because it might not halt.

Here is a connection between the two concepts:

Theorem	A language is recursive if and only if both it and its complement are r.e.

Proof	If the language L is recursive, then so is its complement (by interchanging the accept and reject states of the TM for L). So, one direction of the proof is straightforward.

For the other direction, assume both L and its complement $\bar{L}$ are r.e.; that is, they have TMs. Then run the two machines in *parallel*. At least one of these machines is going to halt, and that gives you the answer.

♦

A **printer Turing machine** is a deterministic TM with an added printer tape. The printer-TM writes a series of strings on the printer tape, separated by some special symbol, such as Δ; once written, a string is not altered. The **output** (or language) of the printer-TM is the set of all strings ever written on the printer tape. The following result is the reason for the terminology "recursively enumerable":

Theorem	A language is r.e. if and only if there is a printer-TM that outputs precisely those strings.

Proof	Armed with a printer-TM M for language L, you can build a normal TM N for L as follows: confronted with input x, the machine N runs M and monitors the output from M; if it ever finds x on the printer tape, it accepts. So, N accepts the strings in L, and does not halt for other strings.

Armed with a normal TM N for L, you can build a printer-TM M for L as follows: the idea is that you run N on every possible string in parallel. The challenge is how to do an infinite number of tasks in parallel and get them all done eventually!

The printer-TM M will work in rounds. In round i, the machine M, starting from scratch, generates the first i strings lexicographically (in dictionary order), runs N on each for i steps, and outputs any string that is accepted. Eventually every string that is in $L(N)$ will be generated and N run for long enough, and hence appear in the output.

♦

13.2 Decidable Questions

Languages are intimately connected with yes/no decision questions. Given a question, you can build a language by taking all the instances of the question where the answer is yes (with the question converted to a string somehow). We say that a yes/no question is **decidable** if the associated language is recursive. Note that this is equivalent to finding a program that always halts and answers the question correctly.

We want to talk about the decidability of questions about TMs, FAs, and so forth. For this, we assume that there is a standard **encoding** of the machine in binary. If the machine is A, then this encoding is written $\langle A \rangle$. This encoding might, for example, be the format you would use to describe a machine if you wrote a Java or C program that was a simulator for that type of machine. It does not matter what the encoding is, as long as it is fixed and you can easily get from the machine to the encoding and back again. We extend this notation; for example, $\langle A, B \rangle$ denotes the encoding of the pair $\{A, B\}$ such that both are reconstructible from the encoding.

13.3 Decidable Questions about Simple Models

It is easy to answer questions about regular languages:

Theorem	Recursive languages are:
	a) The acceptance problem: $A_{fa} = \{\langle M, w \rangle : M$ is FA that accepts $w\}$
	b) The emptiness problem: $Empty_{fa} = \{\langle M \rangle : M$ is FA with empty language$\}$
	c) The equivalence problem: $EQ_{fa} = \{\langle A, B \rangle : A$ and B are FAs with $L(A) = L(B)\}$

Proof

In each case, we build a TM whose first job is to check that the input has the correct syntax. If the input does not have the correct syntax, then the TM rejects. Otherwise, it then does the main work.

In the case of (a), direct simulation will work.

Case (b) is easy. We must check whether there is a path from the start state of M to an accept state: is there an accept state that is reachable? This can be answered with a graph search, such as breadth-first search or depth-first search.

Part (c) asks about testing whether two FAs accept the same language. One approach (though not necessarily quick) is to construct the FA for the following language (also known as the **symmetric difference**):

$$\Delta(A, B) = (L(A) - L(B)) \cup (L(B) - L(A))$$

Then test $\Delta(A, B)$ for emptiness. To build an FA for $L(A) - L(B)$, use the following facts:

$$L(A) - L(B) = \overline{\overline{L(A)} \cup L(B)}$$

by de Morgan's laws; that it is easy to convert a deterministic FA to accept the complement of its language; and that doing the union of two machines is easy with nondeterminism.

◆

Most questions about context-free grammars or languages can be readily answered:

Theorem

Recursive languages are:

a) The acceptance problem: $A_{cfg} = \{ \langle G, w \rangle : G$ is a CFG and w a string of $L(G) \}$
b) Any context-free language with grammar G
c) The emptiness problem: $Empty_{cfg} = \{ \langle G \rangle : L(G)$ is empty $\}$

Proof

Proof sketch

a) For example, convert to Chomsky Normal Form. Examine all derivations of length $2|w| - 1$ and conclude. (This problem was also discussed in Section 10.5.)
b) For example, write G on the tape and pass to program from (a).
c) This was Exercise 8.12.

Surprisingly, perhaps, testing whether a CFG generates every string is hard: $Total_{cfg} = \{\langle G \rangle : L(G) = \Sigma^* \}$ is not recursive. This result will be established in Chapter 15.

13.4 Reasoning about Computation

In proving results about models of computation, it helps to examine the steps involved. Recall that a **configuration**, or snapshot, of a machine is a record of the machine that tells you the state and the contents of memory. The configuration fully captures the current status of the computation.

It follows that, for a deterministic machine, if the same configuration recurs, then the machine is stuck in an infinite loop. Hence, we have a key idea:

Fact	If the number of possible configurations of a deterministic machine is bounded by some quantity Q, and the machine runs for longer than this time Q, then the machine is in an infinite loop.

An example where this is applicable is a machine with a fixed amount of memory.

A **computation string** for machine M accepting string w is the string of configurations from start to finish, separated by some special symbol (for example $'s). Specifically, for our one-tape TM, we write the state where the head is. That is, the configuration is written as

$$t_L \, S \, t_R$$

where t_L is the used tape to the left of the head, S is the current state, and t_R is the used tape to the right of the head.

The following works even if the computation string is for a machine that is nondeterministic.

Fact	For any machine, it is decidable whether a given string is a computation string or not.

Proof	The procedure is to consider the configurations. Check that the first configuration is correct and matches the input; check that each configuration follows from the previous by the rules of the machine; and check that the final configuration is an accepting one.

One of the fundamental questions is how much resources you need to do certain tasks. In particular, the question of how much resources you need to recognize computation strings (or variations) of various models plays a pivotal role.

13.5   Other Models

Recall that we introduced the Chomsky hierarchy in Section 8.2. Though we do not prove it, the top level of the hierarchy corresponds to Turing machines:

Theorem	There is an unrestricted grammar for a language if and only if it is r.e.

Several other models have the same power, including Church's lambda calculus.

There is also a model of computation for context-sensitive grammars. A **linearly bounded automaton** (LBA) is a one-tape TM whose head is not allowed to move off the input portion of the tape (and there is a bell or whistle or whatever that tells it where the tape starts and finishes). Though we do not prove it, it turns out that:

Theorem	There is a nondeterministic LBA for a language if and only if there is a context-sensitive grammar for it.

For You to Do!

1. Show that it is decidable whether an NFA M generates all strings from the alphabet, that is, whether $L(M) = \Sigma^*$.
2. Show that the set of recursive languages is closed under reversal.

EXERCISES

13.1 Let M be an FA and q some state of M. Call q a **useful state** if there exists some input w such that M actually enters q. Let $B = \{ \langle M, q \rangle : q$ is a useful state of $M \}$. Show that B is recursive.

13.2 Let M be an FA. Show that it is decidable whether $L(M)$ is infinite or not.

13.3 Suppose that L is recursive. Describe an enumerator for L^*.

⋆ **13.4** Show that it is decidable whether an RE is the shortest RE that generates that language.

13.5 Describe a printer-TM that enumerates $\{\,a^i b^j : 0 \le i \le j\,\}$.

13.6 Describe a printer-TM that enumerates $\{\,a^{2^n} : n \ge 0\,\}$.

13.7 Let $S = \{\,\langle M \rangle : M$ is a DFA that accepts w^R whenever it accepts $w\,\}$. Show that S is decidable.

⋆ **13.8** Show that the set of recursive languages is closed under union and intersection.

13.9 Describe a TM that enumerates all even-length strings for a unary alphabet.

13.10 Show that if a language is recursive, then there is a printer-TM for it that prints out the language in lexicographic (dictionary) order.

Ⓗ **13.11** Show that if there is a printer-TM that prints out a language in lexicographic (dictionary) order, then the language is recursive.

⋆ **13.12** The **characteristic function** $\chi_L(w)$ of a language L is defined to be 1 if string $w \in L$ and 0 otherwise. Show that the function χ_L is T-computable if and only if the language L is recursive.

13.13 Let L be any r.e. language. We know that there is an unrestricted grammar for L. Show that L can be generated by an unrestricted grammar in which the left side of every production has no terminal.

13.14 Show that if L is accepted by a *nondeterministic* TM that always halts (on any sequence of moves), then L is recursive.

13.15 **a)** Let D be a recursive language of pairs of strings. Let C be the set of all strings x for which there exists some y such that $\langle x, y \rangle \in D$. Show that C is r.e.

b) Let C be an r.e. language. Show that there exists a recursive language D such that C is precisely those strings x such that there exists some y such that $\langle x, y \rangle \in D$.

⋆ **13.16** Show that the set of r.e. languages is closed under the star operation.

13.17 Suppose we have infinitely many r.e. languages $L_1, L_2, \ldots$. Does it follow that their union $\bigcup_{i=1}^{\infty} L_i$ is also r.e.?

13.18 Let language $Right_{tm} = \{\,\langle M, w \rangle : M$ is a TM that when started on input w never moves its head left $\,\}$.

a) Compute a quantity Q such that, if M runs for longer than this time on w without moving its head left, then it will run forever.

b) Use this to show that $Right_{tm}$ is recursive.

13.19 Another definition of an LBA is that it is allowed to move off the input portion of the tape, but there is some constant c that it never visits more than $c(n+1)$ cells for every n and every input of length n. Show that the two definitions are equivalent.

★ **13.20** **a)** Let M be a deterministic LBA with k states and q letters in the tape alphabet, and w an input string of length n. Show that if M computes for longer than $Q = k(n+1)q^{n+1}$ steps, then it will run forever.

   b) Use your answer in the first part to show that the acceptance problem A_{lba} is decidable.

13.21 **a)** Show that if a language A is accepted by a deterministic LBA, then A is accepted by one that always halts. (Hint: Look at the previous two exercises.)

   b) What does this say about the complement of A?

13.22 A 2D-FA is a **two-dimensional finite automaton**: the input is a rectangular array, bounded by some special symbol (say, the blank Δ), and the head can move anywhere in this array (but does not change any symbol). Show that the acceptance problem $A_{2d\text{-}fa}$ is recursive.

"For You to Do" Exercise Solutions

1. One approach is to convert M to a DFA. It is easy to see whether a DFA accepts every string: this happens only if every state is an accept state.

2. The question asks you to show that, if L is recursive, then so is $L^R = \{\, x^R : x \in L \,\}$. If L is decided by TM M, then L^R can be decided by a TM that simply reverses the input string and then calls M.

SUMMARY

A Turing machine (TM) is like an FA, but it has an infinite tape. The input starts on the tape surrounded by blank cells denoted Δ. The program of a TM is represented as a diagram: depending on the symbol under the head and the state, the machine writes a symbol, moves left or right or stays in place, and/or changes state. Once a TM enters the accept state it stops.

A normal TM can simulate a TM with a one-way infinite tape, with multiple tapes, and so forth. A nondeterministic TM is no more powerful than a normal one. Church's thesis says that there is an algorithm for a problem if and only if there is a TM for it. A TM can simulate a normal computer. A universal TM is one that can execute any other TM as an input.

Recursive languages are accepted by TMs that always halt; r.e. languages are accepted by TMs. These two families are closed under intersection and union. If a language is recursive, then so is its complement; if both a language and its complement are r.e., then the language is recursive. There is a connection with printer-TMs.

A problem is decidable if the associated language is recursive. All problems about FAs and REs are decidable; most problems about CFGs and PDAs are decidable. A computation string is a record of the computation of a machine.

Several alternatives to electronic chip-based computers have been proposed. These include quantum and DNA computers, which might soon be realized. However, although they offer the promise of faster computation, they are no more powerful than TMs for solving problems.

Quantum computers use quantum mechanical phenomena to perform calculations in a way different from conventional computers. The idea is that computation can be done with qubits—a qubit can be in a range of states and thus can encode more than one bit of information. These computers are believed, and have been shown in theory, to speed up some calculations such as factoring and searching an array for a number when compared to conventional computers. There are potential applications in cryptography.

DNA computing uses molecules of DNA to compute. The information is encoded as the sequence of base amino acids in the DNA strand. The idea is that by supplying information encoded in strands in two forms, you can exploit the fact that DNA is naturally formed by two very long but self-complementary strands twisted together. The advantage comes from the ability to do multiple calculations simultaneously—massively parallel computation.

We have seen that TMs can do many things. They can certainly simulate a desktop computer, and they can decide questions about FAs and CFGs. We now examine what they cannot do: what questions are undecidable.

The initial proofs of undecidability use a technique called *self-reference*, or *diagonalization*. This is only to get the process started. After that, a technique called *reduction* is used to show that certain problems are undecidable. In particular, we show that you cannot write a program that always halts and takes any program as input and says whether that program halts or not.

Any system that is powerful enough to allow self-reference is going to present problems. Our English language is such a system. Consider for example the **librarian paradox**. Some books mention themselves in the book; many books, especially fiction, do not. An unfortunate library intern is given the task of creating a list of all books in the library that do not mention themselves. She toils all summer. In the end, she has a list. This she triumphantly adds to the reference section as "Non Self-Mentioning Books." She is just about to head back to campus, when the head librarian asks, "Shouldn't that book itself be added to the list?" But when the intern adds it to the list, the book is no longer non-self-mentioning. And yet, if it's not added, it should be added. There is no real solution; it is a paradox.

Accomplishing the impossible means only that the boss will add it to your regular duties. **—Doug Larson**

To infinity . . . and beyond **—Buzz Lightyear**, in **Toy Story**

—No one

This sentence is false.

Don't panic!
—Douglas Adams, **The Hitchhiker's Guide to the Galaxy**

14

Diagonalization and the Halting Problem

Is there for every problem an algorithm? That is, is there some procedure that gives the right answer, is clear and completely described, and is guaranteed to terminate? Is there a TM for every language? It may possibly surprise you that some languages are not recursive. A powerful tool in this area is self-reference. We start by showing this in action. Then, we look at where this idea originated. After that, we get down to proving things are undecidable.

14.1 Self-Denial

The first (admittedly contrived) example of a language that is not recursive is S_{tm}: the self-denying machines. This language is defined as

$$S_{tm} = \{ \langle M \rangle : M \text{ is TM that does not accept } \langle M \rangle \}$$

Note that S_{tm} is a valid language. If we were omniscient, we could see whether a string was in the language by parsing the input w as a TM, and then checking whether that TM accepted w.

Self-denial	S_{tm} is not r.e.

| **Proof** | By contradiction. Suppose there exists a TM that accepts this language; call it M'. Does the machine M' accept $\langle M' \rangle$? Well, $\langle M' \rangle$ is in S_{tm} if and only if $\langle M' \rangle$ does not accept $\langle M' \rangle$. That is, $\langle M' \rangle$ accepts $\langle M' \rangle$ if and only if $\langle M' \rangle$ does not accept $\langle M' \rangle$. A contradiction. Because the logic is correct, the problem must be that the supposition is false: M' does not exist. ♦ |

The preceding proof is actually a form of what is known as a *diagonalization argument* (as will become clear over the next few pages). In fact, we need the result where diagonalization was first used. So let us turn there.

14.2 Countable Sets

What makes two sets the same size? If they are finite, then you can pair the sets off: 10 apples with 10 oranges. This is called a **1–1 correspondence**: every apple and every orange is used up.

Define $\mathbb{N}$ to be the set of all positive integers: $\{1, 2, 3, \dots\}$. What does it mean to be the same size as this set? We immediately run into situations that are perhaps not expected. The even numbers are the same size as $\mathbb{N}$: you can pair 1 with 2, 2 with 4, 3 with 6 and so on. The important fact is that the even numbers are used up:

$$
\begin{array}{ccc}
1 & - & 2 \\
2 & - & 4 \\
3 & - & 6 \\
& \vdots &
\end{array}
$$

A set is defined as **countably infinite** if it is the same size as $\mathbb{N}$. A set is then **countable** if it is finite or countably infinite. This means that you can construct a numbered list of all elements.

We saw already that the even numbers are countable. The integers are countable. The rationals, it turns out, are countable. The mere fact that we bother to define things should make you suspect that there are going to be sets that are not countably infinite. Cantor's great idea was to dare to ask whether everything is countable. . . .

For You to Do!

1. Show that the set of integers, positive and negative, is countable.

14.3 Diagonalization

The diagonalization argument was invented by Cantor around the year 1880. It turns out that both his result and his proof technique are useful to us.

Let's start with the following idea. We show how, given a list of words of the same length, you can always construct a word *that is not on the list*. The idea is to start with the diagonal as a word, and then replace each letter by the next letter in the alphabet. For example:

Example 14.1 Diagonalization

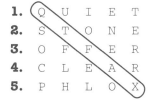

1. Q U I E T
2. S T O N E
3. O F F E R
4. C L E A R
5. P H L O X

In this example, the diagonal string is originally QTFAX, which becomes RUGBY. This word is not on the list.

The point is that the new word *cannot be in the list*; it is different from the first word in the first letter, different from the second word in the second letter, and so forth. Cantor's brilliant insight was that this same idea works with infinite lists.

For a set S, the notation $\mathcal{P}(S)$ is used to denote the set of all subsets of S. All the proofs are by contradiction—we suppose a set has the desired 1–1 correspondence and then produce a contradiction.

Cantor's Theorem The set $\mathcal{P}(\mathbb{N})$ is not countable.

| **Proof** | Suppose $\mathcal{P}(\mathbb{N})$ is countable. What does that mean? That means we can write down a list of all the subsets of $\mathbb{N}$. Maybe it starts: |

$$
\begin{array}{rcl}
1 & - & \mathbb{N} \\
2 & - & \{4, 7\} \\
3 & - & \{2, 4, 6, 8, \dots\} \\
4 & - & \emptyset \\
 & \vdots &
\end{array}
$$

That is, we have a function $f \colon \mathbb{N} \to \mathcal{P}(\mathbb{N})$ that maps numbers to sets such that *every* set appears in the list.

Now, define a set T as follows. For each number i, look up $f(i)$. Add i to the set T exactly when $i \notin f(i)$. This might take us a while, but it certainly is a clear definition of what it takes for a number to be in T. For example, with the above list, 1 is not in T but 2 is.

But, but, but: the set T is not on the list. It's not $f(1)$, because T and $f(1)$ differ on the element 1 (as we defined it such that $1 \in T \iff 1 \notin f(1)$). And it's not $f(2)$, because T and $f(2)$ differ on the element 2. And so on. It is not on the list. That is, f is a lie. It does not use up all the sets in $\mathcal{P}(\mathbb{N})$.

No matter how many times we choose f and make a list, we can still find a set that is not on the list. This contradiction can mean only one thing: such a list does not exist.   ◆

This result has immediate implications for us:

| *Fact* | **1.** For any alphabet, the set of TMs is countable.
2. For any alphabet, the set of languages is uncountable. |

| **Proof** | The set of TMs is countable because each TM can be represented by a binary number and hence as an integer. However, the subsets of the integers are not countable and hence the number of languages is uncountable.   ◆ |

In short, if you pick a language "at random," it stands absolutely no chance of being recursive!

Another version of Cantor's theorem is the following:

Cantor's Theorem revisited	The reals are uncountable.

Proof

Consider only the real numbers at least 0 and less than 1. Each of these can be written as a binary fraction; indeed, by appending 0's, each can be written as an infinite binary expansion.

Suppose you had a list $\mathcal{L}$ of *all* the real numbers between 0 and 1. Say the list $\mathcal{L}$ is $r_1, r_2, \ldots$.

Then, produce a binary expansion ω by the following recipe:

The ith bit of ω is the opposite of the ith bit of r_i.

For example, if the list were as follows, ω would be .10100...:

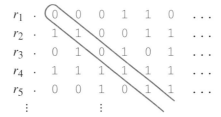

The key point is that ω is the binary expansion of some real number between 0 and 1, but it is **not** on the list. Well, it's not the first number r_1, because they are different in the first bit. It's not r_2, because they are different in the second bit, and so on.

In short, the claim that the list $\mathcal{L}$ is complete is nonsense. And because we can do this trick with any list, there cannot be a list with all binary numbers on it. That is, the set of reals is uncountable.

♦

Here's the diagonalization argument in TMs. Recall that we encode a TM in binary; thus, we can make a list of them in lexicographic (dictionary) order. Now, create a table where each row is labeled by a TM, and each column is labeled by a string that is the encoding of a TM. The entries in the table say whether machine M_i accepts the string $\langle M_j \rangle$ or not.

	$\langle M_0 \rangle$	$\langle M_1 \rangle$	$\langle M_2 \rangle$	$\ldots$
M_0	*Acc*	*Not*	*Not*	
M_1	*Not*	*Not*	*Not*	
M_2	*Not*	*Acc*	*Acc*	
$\vdots$				

Now apply diagonalization; that is, go down the diagonal and change every *Acc* to a *Not* and vice versa. If you write down all those strings that now have an *Acc* on the diagonal, you have a language. This language is precisely—pause for effect—S_{tm}: the self-denying machines.

But this changed diagonal is different from every row. That is, this diagonal behaves differently from every TM. That is, the language is not the language of any TM.

What does this proof approach mean? Although the diagonalization argument does achieve the result—proving something does not exist—we have to acknowledge that it provides limited insight into why something does not exist. This is a shortcoming of nonconstructive proofs.

14.4 The Halting Problem

The language S_{tm} is of little importance. So, consider which problems are of interest. For example, in software engineering it would be useful to know in advance if some code works. Or at least if the program halts. A special case of this is an algorithm that takes as input a TM and a string and that tells you if the TM will halt on that input. One obvious idea is just to use a universal TM. Unfortunately, such an algorithm does not exist, as we now show.

Define $A_{tm} = \{ \langle M, w \rangle : M \text{ is a TM that accepts } w \}$.

Fact	A_{tm} is r.e.

Proof	Simulation: For example, recall the discussion of a universal TM. ◆

We now state the big result:

Theorem	A_{tm} is not recursive. That is, the acceptance problem is undecidable.

The theorem says that you cannot build a TM that will always halt and tell you if a given machine accepts a given string. Using Church's thesis, this means that there does not exist an effective procedure—that is, an algorithm—that you can use to test beforehand if a given machine on a given input will halt.

We give two proofs of the theorem.

Proof 1

The first proof is a direct diagonalization argument: To prove that A_{tm} is undecidable, we "build" a TM D that *for every i* does the opposite of the ith machine on input $\langle M_i \rangle$. So, when we try to find D on our list of all TMs, it is not there!

So, the proof is by contradiction. Suppose there were a machine H that on *every* input $\langle M, w \rangle$ would tell you if M accepted w. Build a new TM D that does the following:

> D: On input w
> 1. Determine the TM S that w encodes.
> 2. Run H on $\langle S, w \rangle$.
> 3. If H accepts, then reject; if H rejects, then accept.

This is a perfectly valid TM. D runs as follows. If the input is not the encoding of a TM, then D rejects. Otherwise, say D has input $\langle S \rangle$. The TM D writes $\langle S, \langle S \rangle \rangle$ on the tape and feeds it into H. It then waits for the answer, and then does the opposite of H.

But wait. What happens to D if the input is the description of D? Say D's input is $w' = \langle D \rangle$ (not that D realizes this). Well, D writes $\langle D, w' \rangle$ on the tape and feeds it to H. If H says accept, then D rejects, and vice versa. That is, if H claims that D accepts $w' = \langle D \rangle$, then D rejects w'. If H says D rejects $w' = \langle D \rangle$, then D accepts w'. Huh?

This is a contradiction, an absurdity. What can be wrong? Everything we did was fine except possibly the fact that H exists. Conclusion: H does not exist.

♦

Proof 2

Suppose there were a TM, call it H, that decided A_{tm}. Then, you could use that machine as a subroutine to decide the language S_{tm}. But that language is not recursive. Contradiction.

♦

The theorem applies to Java, C, and other real programs just as much. It is no easier if all you want to know is if the program will halt—called the halting problem. You can easily adjust a TM so that instead of entering h_r to reject, it instead enters a state that keeps its head moving to the right forever. Solving the halting problem is thus just as hard as solving the acceptance problem. That is, the halting problem is undecidable.

EXERCISES

14.1 Show how diagonalization produces a string not on the following list:

```
E V E R Y
S T A I N
B A C O N
C L I F F
K N E A D
```

14.2 Show that the set of positive rational numbers (the ratios of two positive integers) is countable.

14.3 Is each of the following countable or uncountable?

   a) The set of all functions from $\mathbb{N}$ to $\{0, 1\}$
   b) The set of all functions from $\{0, 1\}$ to $\mathbb{N}$
   c) The set of all functions from $\mathbb{N}$ to $\mathbb{N}$

★ **14.4** Show that any infinite r.e. set has an infinite recursive subset.

14.5 Define $A_{lba} = \{\langle M, w \rangle : M$ is an LBA that accepts $w\}$. Show that the acceptance problem A_{lba} is not decidable by an LBA.

14.6 A k-PDA is a nondeterministic pushdown automaton with k stacks. So, a 0-PDA is an NFA, a 1-PDA is a conventional PDA, and so forth. Determine the power of a 2-PDA. (2-PDAs were considered in Exercise 12.24.)

H **14.7** Write a program whose output is a copy of itself. (And the Basic program "list" does not count!) For example, in English you might write the following:

```
Print out two copies of the following sentence, the second one in quotes.
"Print out two copies of the following sentence, the second one in quotes."
```

14.8 (TERM PAPER) "The limits of computation were determined even before the possibilities of computation." Discuss with specific reference to the work of Cantor, Turing, Church, and Gödel.

"For You to Do" Exercise Solutions

   1. Use the 1–1 correspondence: $1 : 0$, $2 : 1$, $3 : -1$, $4 : 2$, $5 : -2$. That is, $f(i) = i/2$ if i is even, and $f(i) = -(i-1)/2$ if i is odd.

15

More Undecidable Problems

The general tool for proving questions undecidable is to use what is called a reduction. We show that answering the new question would enable us to decide a question we already know is undecidable.

15.1 Reductions

In the second proof of the undecidability of the halting problem in Chapter 14, we used the fact that one language was not decidable to prove that another language was not decidable. This technique is very common. Let's formalize it.

Recall that a T-computable function is a function from strings to strings for which there is a TM. Let A, B be languages. We say that A is **reducible** to B, written $A \leq_m B$, if there is a T-computable function f such that $w \in A$ exactly when $f(w) \in B$. Some say that f *preserves membership*. (The m in $\leq_m$ stands for mapping.)

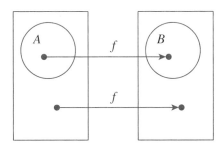

The importance of such a reduction is that answering questions about B is enough to answer questions about A.

Fact	**a)** If A is reducible to B and B is recursive, then A is recursive.
	b) If A is reducible to B and A is not recursive, then B is not recursive.

Proof	(a) Let TM R decide language B, and let function f reduce A to B. Construct TM S as follows: on input w, it computes $f(w)$ and submits this to R; then it accepts if and only if R accepts. So, S decides A.
	Part (b) actually says the same thing as Part (a). ♦

A similar result holds for r.e. languages. This fact explains the notation $\leq_m$ as less-than-or-equal: if $A \leq_m B$, then B is at least as hard as A. This relationship behaves as you would expect. For example:

Fact	For any languages A, B, and C: if $A \leq_m B$ and $B \leq_m C$, then $A \leq_m C$.

Proof	Assume function f reduces A to B and function g reduces B to C. Then the function h, which is defined by $h(w) = g(f(w))$, is a reduction from A to C. The string w is in A exactly when $f(w)$ is in B; the string $f(w)$ is in B exactly when $g(f(w))$ is in C. ♦

 For You to Do!   **1.** Show that for any languages A and B: if $A \leq_m B$, then $\bar{A} \leq_m \bar{B}$.

15.2 Questions about TMs

Here is the idea of reduction used to prove that questions about TMs are undecidable.

Example 15.1   Consider the problem of determining whether a TM on input w ever enters a particular state q.

We reduce the acceptance problem A_{tm} to this problem (call it the **state-use** problem). Suppose you have an algorithm for the state-use problem. Then, you can modify it into an algorithm for the acceptance problem. The idea is to take the input $\langle M, w \rangle$ to the acceptance problem. Then introduce a new state q' and adjust M so that any transition leading to the accept state h_a leads to q' instead. Then, answering the question of whether M uses q' on w is equivalent to answering the question of whether M accepts w. This we know is undecidable.

Example 15.2   Even determining whether a machine accepts the blank tape is impossible: $A_{bt} = \{ \langle M \rangle : M \text{ accepts } \varepsilon \}$ is not recursive.

The proof is to reduce A_{tm} to A_{bt}. That is, given a TM M and a string w, you build a new TM M_w. The reduction f is given by $f(\langle M, w \rangle) = \langle M_w \rangle$. The TM M_w is programmed to do the following:

1. Erase its input
2. Write w on the tape
3. Pass it to M
4. Accept exactly when M accepts

So, M_w accepts ε exactly when $\langle M, w \rangle \in A_{tm}$. Hence, if you could answer questions about A_{bt}, you would be able to answer questions about A_{tm}, which we know is undecidable.

Here is a visualization. The outer box does A_{tm} if we have a decider for A_{bt}.

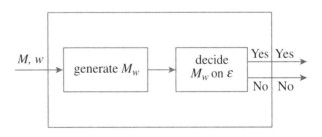

(It almost sounds like we're cheating.)

For You to Do!

2. Show that it is undecidable whether a TM ever writes a particular symbol on the tape.

Actually, most questions about TMs are undecidable.

> *Rice's Theorem* Any question about r.e. languages that is nontrivial is undecidable.

By **nontrivial** we mean there is some language for which the answer is "yes" and some for which the answer is "no." We omit the beautiful but simple reduction that does this.

15.3 Other Machines

We saw earlier that you can answer several questions about context-free languages. We now show, however, that the totality problem is undecidable. We need the fact that a PDA can decide whether one configuration follows from another.

> *Fact* Given a deterministic TM M, you can build a deterministic PDA that accepts the following language: $\{c_1^R \# c_2 : c_1, c_2$ are configurations of M such that c_2 follows from $c_1\}$.

Proof The PDA starts by pushing the first configuration c_1 onto the stack; this unreverses c_1. Then, as it reads in the second configuration c_2, the PDA compares them. The two configurations are largely identical except for the patch around the state symbol. So, the PDA reads one symbol at a time, popping a symbol, checking that they match, and discarding. It does this until it hits the first state symbol, either on the stack or in the input.

The PDA then checks whether the implied transition is correct according to the rules of M. For example, suppose the stack top is the state B and the symbol 0 is read. Then, pop another symbol—say, it's 1—and read another symbol—it should be a state symbol, say, state C.

This situation corresponds to the transition $\delta(B, 1) = (C, 0, \text{R})$. So, the PDA checks that that is one of the transitions of M (M is hard-coded into the PDA).

If it passes the test for the patch around the state symbol, then the PDA reads and pops to the end, checking that the symbols match as before.

♦

Theorem	It is undecidable whether a PDA accepts every string.

Proof   The basic idea is to reduce from A_{tm} by designing a PDA that accepts all strings that are **not** "computation strings." The key idea here is that

nondeterminism simplifies checking that the string is invalid because you have to find only one flaw.

We saw earlier that to check whether a given string is a computation string for M on w entails checking three things: that the first configuration is correct; that the last configuration is accepting; and that every configuration follows from the previous one.

For $\langle M, w \rangle$, define the language of altered computation strings:

$$N_{M,w} = \{\, c_1 \# c_2^R \# c_3 \# c_4^R \# \ldots \# c_k \,\}$$

where c_1 is the start configuration, c_k is an accepting configuration, and each c_i follows from c_{i-1}. That is, the configurations are written down with every second one reversed. We will build a PDA $P_{M,w}$ for the *complement* of $N_{M,w}$.

This PDA will guess one of three flaws to find: that the first configuration is wrong, that the last configuration is not accepting, or that somewhere one configuration does not follow from the previous one. The first two of these are easy for $P_{M,w}$ to check: for a string in $N_{M,w}$, the first configuration should be $q_0 w$; and the last configuration should be accepting, that is, its state should be h_a.

For the third flaw, the PDA uses nondeterminism to guess which pair of configurations is in conflict. Having guessed which pair to check, we saw in the previous fact that a PDA can do the checking. The PDA $P_{M,w}$ accepts whenever it finds a problem: that the first or last configuration is wrong, or that some configuration does not follow from the previous one.

Now for the punch line: if M does not accept w, then there is no real computation string. That is, $N_{M,w}$ is empty. Hence $P_{M,w}$ accepts every string. If M does accept w, then there is a real computation string and so

$P_{M,w}$ does not accept every string. That is, being able to answer the totality question for PDAs would enable us to answer the acceptance question for TMs. Because the latter is undecidable, so is the former.

♦

15.4 Post's Correspondence Problem

Here is another famous undecidable question. In the problem, you are given a set of tiles: each tile has a top string and a bottom string. A **solution** is to choose a subset of the tiles and order them such that the string reading across the top is the same as the string reading across the bottom. This is called Post's Correspondence Problem (PCP).

Example 15.3 Suppose the tiles are $(0, 101)$, $(10101, 10)$, $(11, 00000)$, and $(1, 01)$. Then, one solution is:

10101	0	1
10	101	01

Well how hard can that be?

Define **modified PCP** (MPCP) as a PCP problem where one tile is designated the start tile.

Theorem A_{tm} reduces to MPCP. Hence, MPCP is undecidable.

Proof   ROUGH PROOF SKETCH: Consider a $\langle M, w \rangle$ that might be in A_{tm}. The idea is

to design a set of tiles such that a solution to the tiles is a computation string for M on w.

That is, as you read across the top or bottom, you see a sequence of *configurations* of the TM leading to acceptance. In what follows, we give just the outline of how to build the set of tiles, and do not attempt to prove that this works.

Recall that a configuration of a TM is written as $t_L\, S\, t_R$ where t_L is the used tape to the left of the head, S the current state, and t_R the used tape to the right of the head. So, the start configuration is $q_0 w$. The solution will be such that for the most part the bottom of the solution is one configuration ahead of the top of the solution.

These are five kinds of tiles:

- The start tile is defined to be $(\$, \$q_0 w\$)$ where $\$$ is a special symbol.
- For the tiles that describe the action of the machine, we iterate through the transitions: if q is a state and b a symbol in the tape alphabet, then

  - If $\delta(q, b) = (r, \text{c}, \text{L})$, then add tiles $(\text{a}q\text{b}, r\text{ac})$ for all symbols a.
  - If $\delta(q, b) = (r, \text{c}, \text{R})$, then add tile $(q\text{b}, \text{c}r)$.

- We also need to deal with the machine moving to a cell not previously visited. For this, we add the tiles $(\$, \triangle\$)$ and $(\$, \$\triangle)$.
- To allow for the copying down of the rest of the configuration, add tiles that read (a, a) for every symbol.
- Finally, we add tiles that allow the top row to catch up provided that the bottom row has reached the accept state h_a. For every symbol b in the tape alphabet, add tiles $(\text{b}h_a, h_a)$, $(h_a\text{b}, h_a)$, and $(h_a\$, \varepsilon)$.

Apart from the start tile, there are unlimited copies of each tile.

Note that only the last group of tiles has a bottom that is shorter than the top. So, for a solution to occur, you must have gotten to the accept state in a legitimate way.

The fundamental point is that there is a solution to the resultant MPCP exactly when the TM accepts the input string. Because the latter is undecidable, so is the former.

A formal proof that the set of tiles has the desired property can be done using mathematical induction, but we omit this.

♦

One can also show that MPCP reduces to PCP; this is more a trick (see the exercises).

EXERCISES

15.1 Give short justifications of these facts about $\leq_m$. For any language B:

- **a)** If B is r.e. and $B \leq_m \bar{B}$, then B is recursive.
- **b)** If B is recursive, then $B \leq_m \text{a}^*\text{b}^*$.
- **c)** If B is r.e., then $B \leq_m A_{tm}$.

15.2 Consider the language $Left_{tm} = \{ \langle M, w \rangle : M$ moves to the cell off the left end of input $w \}$. Show that this language is not recursive.

15.3 Show that it is undecidable if the language of a TM is empty.

★ **15.4** Show that it is undecidable if every string in the language of a TM has even length.

15.5 Show that it is undecidable if two TMs accept the same language.

15.6 Show that it is undecidable if the language of a TM is regular.

15.7 Show that it is undecidable if a CFG generates every string.

★ **15.8** Show that is is undecidable if two CFGs generate the same language.

15.9 From Exercise 13.22. Show that testing if the language of a 2D-FA is nonempty is undecidable. (Hint: Consider a 2D-FA that accepts Turing "computation rectangles.")

15.10 Show that $Empty_{lba}$ is not decidable. (Hint: Given a $\langle M, w \rangle$, build an LBA $B_{M,w}$ that accepts only valid computation strings for M accepting w.)

15.11 Show that MPCP reduces to PCP. (Hint: Introduce a special symbol into the tiles.)

★ **15.12** Show that PCP with a *unary* alphabet is decidable.

"For You to Do" Exercise Solutions

1. The same reduction works! If function f reduces A to B, then it maps A to B and $\bar{A}$ to $\bar{B}$.

2. Assume we are given some TM M and string w. Construct a new machine M_w. The TM M_w is programmed to erase its input, write w on the tape, and pass this over to M. If M accepts, then M_w writes a special symbol, say \$, on the tape. Thus, if you could answer the question whether M_w writes \$ or not, you would be able to decide A_{tm}, which is undecidable.

16

Recursive Functions

An alternative to Turing machines is the concept of recursive functions. These deal with integers rather than strings. We can easily convert between integers and strings; indeed, a computer often does so. By extension, because information and algorithms are encoded as strings, we can encode them as numbers. This was brilliantly exploited by Gödel when he proved certain impossibility results about proving things. Read about them! Here we provide only a brief introduction to recursive function theory, omitting several proofs.

16.1 Primitive Recursive Functions

Suppose we need to produce the nonnegative integers. All good things come from a start. The start here is zero.

What is the idea? Well, 0 exists. It has a successor 1. Which has a successor 2. And so on. So, let us define the **successor** operator: the function $S(x)$ that takes a number x to its successor $x + 1$. This gives us the nonnegative integers $\mathbb{N}_0 = \{0, 1, 2, \dots\}$.

To do things with $\mathbb{N}_0$, we need operations. For example, how to define addition? This must be in terms of the successor function because initially that is all we have. Here is a recursive definition of addition:

$$add(x, 0) = x$$
$$add(x, S(y)) = S(add(x, y))$$

Does this work? Yes, this gives a clear recipe. For example, we can show that $2 + 2 = 4$:

$$
\begin{aligned}
add(2,2) &= S(add(2,1)) \\
&= S(S(add(2,0))) \\
&= S(S(2)) \\
&= S(3) \\
&= 4
\end{aligned}
$$

We now try to formalize the rules for the preceding process. First, all values in sight are in $\mathbb{N}_0$. Unless otherwise specified, a function is defined for all of $\mathbb{N}_0$ (a **total** function). To simplify presentation we restrict attention to functions that have one or two variables.

Primitive recursive functions are built up from three basic functions using two operations. The basic functions are as follows:

1. **Zero.** The zero function $Z(x) \equiv 0$.
2. **Successor.** The successor function $S(x) \equiv x + 1$.
3. **Projection.** A projection function selects out one of the arguments. Specifically,

$$
P_1(x, y) \equiv x \qquad and \qquad P_2(x, y) \equiv y
$$

There are two operations that make new functions from old:

1. **Composition.** Composition replaces the arguments of a function with other functions. For example, you can define a function f by

$$
f(x, y) = g(h_1(x, y), h_2(x, y))
$$

where you supply the functions h_1, h_2, and g. We used this in the definition of add.
2. **Primitive recursion.** Primitive recursion allows you to make more complex functions. A typical use of primitive recursion has the following form:

$$
\begin{aligned}
f(x, 0) &= g_1(x) \\
f(x, S(y)) &= h(g_2(x, y), f(x, y))
\end{aligned}
$$

where you supply the functions g_1, g_2, and h. For example, in the case of addition, the h is the successor function of the projection of the second argument. Note that you are allowed to recurse on only the last argument.

A special case of primitive recursion is for some constant number k:

$$f(0) = k$$
$$f(S(y)) = h(y, f(y))$$

Primitive recursive functions	A function is primitive recursive if it can be built up using the base functions and the operations of composition and primitive recursion.

It should be clear that composition and primitive recursion preserve the property of being computable by a TM. For example, in the previous special case of primitive recursion, to calculate $f(5)$, the obvious algorithm computes $f(4)$, by recursion, and then computes $h(4, f(4))$. That is:

Fact	A primitive recursive function is T-computable.

16.2 Examples: Functions and Predicates

Let's look at some more examples of primitive recursive functions.

Example 16.1	**Multiplication.** The obvious attempt does the trick:

$$mul(x, 0) = 0$$
$$mul(x, S(y)) = add(x, mul(x, y))$$

To simplify notation, now that we have shown that addition and multiplication are primitive recursive functions, we use normal arithmetical notation for them.

Subtraction is harder. First, we need to stay within the domain $\mathbb{N}_0$. So, we define "subtract as much as you can," called **monus**. This operation is commonly written as $\dot{-}$ and is defined by:

$$x \dot{-} y = \begin{cases} x - y & \text{if } x \geq y, \\ 0 & \text{otherwise.} \end{cases}$$

To formulate monus as a primitive recursive function, we need the concept of predecessor.

| Example 16.2 | Predecessor. |

$$pred(0) = 0$$
$$pred(S(y)) = y$$

 For You to Do!   **1.** Show that monus is primitive recursive.

| Example 16.3 | What about the zero-recognizer function? This is a function that is 1 for the argument 0, and 0 otherwise. Well, here is a formula: |

$$sgn(0) = 1$$
$$sgn(S(y)) = 0$$

A function that takes on only the values 0 and 1 can be thought of as a **predicate**: something that is either true or false, where 0 means false, and 1 means true.

| Example 16.4 | Suppose $a(x)$ is a primitive recursive predicate. Then how about the opposite? "Not a," so to speak. Well, $na(x) = 1 - a(x)$. |

| Example 16.5 | Defining a function using a **case statement**: |

$$f(x) = \begin{cases} g(x) \text{ if } p(x), \\ h(x) \text{ otherwise.} \end{cases}$$

We claim that if g and h are primitive recursive functions, then f is primitive recursive, too. One way to see this is to write some algebra:

$$f(x) \equiv g(x)\, p(x) + (1 - p(x))\, h(x)$$

Note that the formula simplifies to $g(x)$ if $p(x) = 1$, and to $h(x)$ if $p(x) = 0$.

For You to Do!

2. Show that if $p(x)$ and $q(x)$ are primitive recursive predicates, then so is $p \wedge q$ (the and of them) defined to be true exactly when both $p(x)$ and $q(x)$ are true.

16.3 Functions That Are Not Primitive Recursive

Theorem   Not all T-computable functions are primitive recursive.

Proof   Yes, it's a diagonalization argument. Each partial recursive function is given by a finite string. Therefore, you can number them $f_1, f_2, \ldots$. Define a function g by

$$g(x) = f_x(x) + 1$$

This g is a perfectly computable function. But it cannot be primitive recursive for the same old1reason: it is different from each primitive recursive function.   ◆

Actually, the primitive recursive functions can be shown to correspond to those functions that can be computed using only loops of fixed length.

There is a famous specific example of a function that is not primitive recursive: **Ackermann's function**. This function is very fast growing. In fact, it grows faster than any primitive recursive function does. Ackermann's function is defined by

$$A(0, y) = y + 1$$
$$A(x, 0) = A(x - 1, 1)$$
$$A(x, y + 1) = A(x - 1, A(x, y))$$

Example 16.6   Here are some very small values of Ackermann's function:
$$A(1, 0) = A(0, 1) = 2$$
$$A(1, 1) = A(0, A(1, 0)) = A(0, 2) = 3$$
$$A(1, 2) = A(0, A(1, 1)) = A(0, 3) = 4$$

$$A(2,0) = A(1,1) = 3$$
$$A(2,1) = A(1, A(2,0)) = A(1,3) = A(0, A(1,2)) = A(0,4) = 5$$

This definition gives us a formula. It is not a primitive recursive formula as it stands, but that does not by itself mean it cannot be massaged into one. Nevertheless, it can be shown that Ackermann's function is not primitive recursive.

For You to Do!   **3.** Calculate $A(2,2)$.

16.4   Bounded and Unbounded Minimization

In this section, we give a characterization of which functions are T-computable. This is based on the operation where one function is defined to be the smallest value such that something is true.

Suppose $q(x,y)$ is some predicate. One operation is called **bounded minimization**. This typically looks like the following. For fixed number k:

$$f(x) = \min\{\, y \le k : q(x,y) \,\}$$

Note that you have to deal with those x where there is no y—let's define $f(x)$ as k in that case. Actually, bounded minimization is just an extension of the case statement (equivalent to $k-1$ nested case statements), and so it is not surprising then that the following is true:

Fact   If f is formed by bounded minimization from a primitive recursive predicate, then f is primitive recursive.

Proof   This has an algebraic proof. Let's abbreviate $r_x(y) = 1 - q(x,y)$. Then,

$$f(x) \equiv \sum_{u=0}^{k} \prod_{y=0}^{u} r_x(y)$$

Okay, this is mathematical notation at its finest—beautiful if you're used to it, horrible if you're not. The formula says that $f(x)$ is equivalent to a *sum of products.* For example, if $k = 3$, this formula is $r_x(0) + r_x(0)r_x(1) + r_x(0)r_x(1)r_x(2) + r_x(0)r_x(1)r_x(2)r_x(3)$.

Well, let's check the formula. If $r_x(0) = 0$—meaning $q(x, 0)$ is true—then every term in the sum is zero, so that the formula gives $f(x) = 0$, as required. If $r_x(0) = r_x(1) = 1$ and $r_x(2) = 0$, then only the terms $r_x(0)$ and $r_x(0)r_x(1)$ evaluate to 1, so that the formula gives $f(x) = 2$, as required. Think about the case $k = 3$ yourself.

Once you accept the formula, then because addition and multiplication are primitive recursive, it follows that so is f.

◆

You may suspect the same is true of unbounded minimization. But then again, the fact that we separate this out should suggest something's afoot. We define

$$f(x) = \mu\, q(x, y)$$

to mean that $f(x)$ is the minimum y such that the predicate $q(x, y)$ is true (and $f(x) = 0$ if $q(x, y)$ is always false).

Definition   A function is μ-**recursive** if it can be built up using the base functions and the operations of composition, primitive recursion, and unbounded minimization.

It is not hard to believe that all such functions can be computed by some TM. What is a much deeper result is that every TM function corresponds to some μ-recursive function.

Theorem   A function is T-computable if and only if it is μ-recursive.

We omit the proof.

EXERCISES

16.1 Show that the following functions are primitive recursive:

  a) $f(x) = 27$
  b) $f(x) + g(x)$ given that f and g are primitive recursive

16.2 Show that the following functions are primitive recursive:

  a) The factorial function $n!$
  b) $f(x) = 2x$
  c) Permuting the variables: $f(x, y) = g(y, x)$ where g is primitive recursive

16.3 Show that the following predicates are primitive recursive:

   a) Equals
   b) Less than or equal
   c) The characteristic function of a fixed finite set X: it should be 1 for members of X and 0 otherwise.

★ **16.4** Write the maximum of two values x and y as an expression involving the monus function. Hence, show that the maximum function $m(x, y)$ is primitive recursive.

16.5   **a)** The function $mod(x, y)$ is defined as the remainder when x is divided by y. (For completeness define it as zero if y is zero.) Show that mod is primitive recursive.

   b) The function $quot(x, y)$ is defined as the quotient when x is divided by y. (Again, define it as zero if y is zero.) Show that $quot$ is primitive recursive.

16.6 Write a program to compute Ackermann's function. Use it to determine $A(3, 6)$ and $A(4, 1)$.

16.7 Prove the following facts about Ackermann's function:

   a) $A(1, y) = y + 2$
   b) $A(2, y) = 2y + 3$
   c) $A(3, y) = 2^{y+3} - 3$
   d) $A(4, y) = 2^{2^{\cdot^{\cdot^{\cdot^2}}}} - 3$ where there are $y + 3$ *two*'s in that tower.

16.8 (TERM PAPER) "Universal TMs and the Busy Beaver problem"

16.9 (TERM PAPER) "Gödel, Gödel numbering, and Incompleteness Theorems"

"For You to Do" Exercise Solutions

1. Using the predecessor function:

$$sub(x, 0) = x$$
$$sub(x, S(y)) = pred(sub(x, y))$$

2. $p \wedge q = p(x) \times q(x)$

3. $A(2, 2) = A(1, A(2, 1)) = A(1, 5) = A(0, A(1, 4))$.

   Now, $A(1, 4) = A(0, A(1, 3))$, and $A(1, 3) = A(0, A(1, 2)) = A(0, 4) = 5$.

   So, $A(1, 4) = 6$, and $A(2, 2) = 7$.

SUMMARY

A set is countable if it can be placed in 1–1 correspondence with the positive integers. Cantor showed by diagonalization that the set of subsets of the integers is not countable, as is the set of infinite binary sequences. Every TM has an encoding as a finite binary string. Because there is a canonical ordering of binary strings, an infinite language corresponds to an infinite binary sequence. Hence, almost all languages are not r.e.

The language S_{tm} (self-denial) is not r.e. The acceptance language A_{tm} and hence the halting problem are r.e. but not recursive. The proof uses self-reference.

A reduction is a mapping that preserves membership. A reduction can be used to show that one problem is undecidable given the undecidability of another problem. Several problems about TMs are proven undecidable by reduction from the acceptance problem A_{tm}. This approach also shows that determining if a PDA accepts all strings is undecidable, as is Post's Correspondence Problem (PCP).

A primitive recursive function is built up from the base functions zero, successor, and projection using the two operations composition and primitive recursion. There are T-computable functions that are not primitive recursive, such as Ackermann's function.

Who were these people? Alan Turing (1912–1954) is regarded by some as the father of computer science. He is famous both for his formal model of computation, the Turing machine, but also for his discussion about the possibility of artificial intelligence and his proposal of a Turing test to measure this. During World War II, he was significant in Britain's codebreaking effort at Bletchley Park and helped design an electromechanical computer. He later contributed to the design of other early computers.

Alonzo Church (1903–1995) spent much of his working career at Princeton, where he contributed greatly to the development of logic. He invented lambda calculus, a more mathematical formalization of an algorithm, and showed that this had the same power as the Turing machine. He was also Turing's PhD advisor.

The German, Georg Cantor (1845–1918), was one of the main developers of set theory. His proof that the real numbers are uncountable was published in the late 1800s. The idea of multiple infinities and the paradoxes that go with them did not sit well with many mathematicians.

The American, Emil Post (1897–1954), made fundamental contributions in logic. Apart from independently creating a computer model with the same power as Turing, he recognized the utility of truth tables for manipulating logical expressions.

Kurt Gödel (1906–1978) is most famous for his incompleteness theorems. Essentially, he showed that no matter what collection of axioms you write down for mathematics, there will always be statements that are true but not provable. One of his fundamental tools was the idea that a single number can encode a statement or formula; this Gödel numbering is used, for example, in proving results about recursive functions.

part
V

Complexity Theory

The field of **computational complexity** looks at the resources required to solve problems. For example, how fast you can solve a certain type of problem. Or, more generally, how much resources does it take: time, memory space, number of processors, bandwidth, and so forth. It is a given that the problem is solvable.

As regards time, we define two sets of languages. The set $\mathcal{P}$ is those languages (or decision problems) that can be solved in polynomial time, and $\mathcal{NP}$ is the set of those languages that can be solved in polynomial time on a nondeterministic TM. The set $\mathcal{P}$ is somewhat viewed as the reasonably tractable problems, but a myriad of problems of practical interest have been shown to be in $\mathcal{NP}$. Thus, the question of whether all of $\mathcal{NP}$ is in $\mathcal{P}$ (that is, whether $\mathcal{P} = \mathcal{NP}$) is of fundamental importance. Unfortunately, this question remains unresolved.

We also discuss the memory-space requirements of problems and the relationship between time and space. We also consider evidence that certain problems in $\mathcal{NP}$ are indeed hard.

Nothing puzzles me more than time and space; and yet nothing troubles me less, as I never think about them. —**Charles Lamb**

Prose, aiming at a definite and concrete goal, generally suppresses everything inessential to its purpose; poetry, existing only to exhibit itself as an aesthetic object, aims only at completeness and perfection of form. —**Richard Fogle**

Mathematics alone make us feel the limits of our intelligence. —**Simone Weil**

Theory can leave questions unanswered, but practice has to come up with something. —**Mason Cooley**

chapter
17

Time Complexity

The most common resource is time. The **time complexity** of a set of problems is how much time is needed to solve them. Equivalently, the time complexity of a language is how much time is needed to decide membership in it.

17.1 Time

The goal is to determine how the resources required depend on the size of the input. For example, sorting a list of 2 elements is clearly going to be quicker than sorting a list of 2 million elements. The question is: How much quicker? To quantify this, n always denotes the size of the input. Then, the running time is the number of steps as a function of n.

Example 17.1 Consider a TM that decides the language E of binary strings with an equal number of 0's and 1's. The simplest idea is to cross off the first symbol. Say it is a 1. Then, go and find the first 0 and cross it off. Then, come back to the first unmarked symbol. And so forth. The machine accepts if the 0's run out at the same time as the 1's. This TM was drawn in Figure 11.1.

If the input has length n, then the time taken could be as high as about $n^2/4$ steps ($n/2$ iterations with average length $n/2$). The time taken is **quadratic** in the length of the input: proportional to n^2.

It is important to note that we analyze the **worst case**. It doesn't matter that some instances can be done quickly; what matters is if *every* instance can be done quickly. Indeed, a TM is said to run in time $T(n)$ if, for all inputs w, it halts within $T(|w|)$ steps.

Further, it is important to note that *constants do not matter*. If a machine runs in $2n^2$, $7n^2$, or $1000n^2$ steps is immaterial. In fact, we *cannot* care about the constants. For, the exact time will depend very heavily on what the atomic operations are. And nobody uses a laptop TM anyway. So, we say that the preceding TM runs in $O(n^2)$ time, or "order n^2" time, meaning there exists some constant c such that the TM runs in at most cn^2 steps for *any* input of length n. The order notation, also known as big-O notation, says how the worst-case running time grows as n gets large.

Example 17.1 (continued) | Can we improve on the previous program? Well, if there are two tapes, you can do as follows: Make two copies of the input. Then, run the heads along both strings, matching the 0's and 1's. Such a machine accepts E and takes linear time, meaning $O(n)$ steps. It is left as an exercise to show that you can decide the preceding language E with a 1-tape TM in $O(n \log n)$ time. (And this is best possible, but that's much harder to prove.)

So, the model of computation matters. In what follows

we will assume a multitape TM.

It can be shown that a 2-tape TM can simulate any multitape TM while only increasing the running time by a constant factor. For example, it follows that the language PALIN of all palindromes is decidable in $O(n)$ time. So is the language E from Example 17.1.

17.2 Polynomial Time

We turn now to the definition of $\mathcal{P}$:

> The collection of all problems that can be solved in polynomial time is called $\mathcal{P}$.

That is, a language L is in $\mathcal{P}$ if there is a constant k and a TM that decides L that runs in time $O(n^k)$.

It is common to call a set of related languages a **complexity class** or just a class. The class $\mathcal{P}$ roughly captures the collection of practically solvable problems. Or at least that is the conventional wisdom. Something that runs in time 2^n requires double the time if you add one symbol to the input. Something that runs in polynomial time does not suffer from this problem.

The class $\mathcal{P}$ is robust in the sense that any two reasonable deterministic models of computation give rise to the same definition of $\mathcal{P}$. We can make this statement slightly more precise:

Definition	Two models of computation are **polynomially related** if there is a polynomial p such that if a language is decidable in time $T(n)$ on one model, then it is decidable in time $p(T(n))$ on the other.

Example 17.2	A k-tape TM and a 1-tape TM are polynomially related. Why? A 1-tape TM can simulate a k-tape TM by, for example, writing the contents of the k tapes next to each other on its tape. How long does this simulation take? Well, each of the $T(n)$ steps of the k-tape TM requires the 1-tape TM to traverse the length of the tape. How long can each string on the k-tape get? At most $T(n)$. So, the simulation takes at most $O((T(n))^2)$ time, the square of $T(n)$.

One important case is that a TM is polynomially related to a "standard computer," where a standard computer is defined as a device that has finite internal memory, fixed word length, and fixed instruction set and that can access a bounded amount of external memory at one step. It follows that the class $\mathcal{P}$ is the same whether we think in terms of TMs or of normal computer algorithms.

17.3 Examples

Example 17.3	**Sorting.** Note that we are still dealing with languages, or equivalently, yes–no questions. So, the question for sorting is how to check if an input list is sorted. This problem can clearly be solved in linear time by comparing each entry with the next.

Questions about logic are important. A **boolean formula** consists of variables and negated variables (known collectively as **literals**), and the operations *and* and *or*. We use $\vee$ for *or*, $\wedge$ for *and*, and $\bar{x}$ for *not* x. For example:

$$x \wedge (x \vee y \vee \bar{z}) \wedge (\bar{x} \vee \bar{y})$$

An **assignment** is a setting of each of the variables to either TRUE or FALSE. For example, if x and y are TRUE and z is FALSE, then the preceding boolean formula is FALSE.

Example 17.4

TRUEBF $= \{ \langle \phi, \psi \rangle : \phi$ is boolean formula made TRUE by assignment $\psi \}$.

A boolean formula can be parsed and evaluated like a normal arithmetic expression using a single stack. Indeed, given a boolean function and an assignment of the variables, we can determine if the formula is TRUE in linear time. It follows that the language TRUEBF is in $\mathcal{P}$.

We also use graph-theory questions as examples because they are often the most natural and accessible questions. A **graph** consists of a set of **nodes** and a set of **edges**. Each edge joins two nodes. Two nodes that are joined by an edge are said to be **adjacent**.

A **path** is a sequence of edges leading from one node to another. A **Hamiltonian path** from node a to node b in a graph is a path from a to b that visits every node exactly once.

Example 17.5

In the graph drawn, there is a path from every node to every other node. There is a Hamiltonian path from A to I (visiting the nodes in alphabetical order). But there is not a Hamiltonian path from A to C.

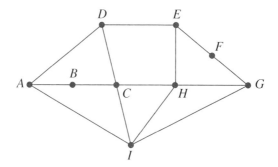

Example 17.6

PATH $= \{\, \langle G, a, b \rangle : G$ is a graph with path from a to $b \,\}$.

This language is in $\mathcal{P}$. To see if there is a path from node a to node b, you might determine all the nodes reachable from a by doing, for instance, a breadth-first search. Note that the actual running time depends on the representation of the graph.

Example 17.7

What about a context-free language L? The CYK algorithm (Section 10.5) shows that any context-free language can be decided reasonably quickly. We did not do the analysis, but the running time of the CYK algorithm is $O(n^3)$. Thus, $L \in \mathcal{P}$.

17.4 Nondeterministic Time

For a nondeterministic TM, like for an NFA, you obtain a computation tree. Recall that an NTM M decides a language A if for every input w, all branches of M halt, and w is in A exactly when there is some accepting branch. The time taken by M is the length of the *longest* branch.

> The collection of all problems that can be solved in polynomial time by a nondeterministic machine is called $\mathcal{NP}$.

That is, a language L is in $\mathcal{NP}$ if there is a constant k and an NTM that decides L that runs in time $O(n^k)$. It should be immediate that

$$\mathcal{P} \subseteq \mathcal{NP}$$

Does nondeterminism buy us anything? It didn't with FAs or TMs, but it did with PDAs. So, the only thing the previous parts of the book should convince you of is that it could go either way here.

Example 17.8

HAMPATH $= \{\, \langle G, a, b \rangle : G$ is graph with hamiltonian path from a to $b \,\}$.

It is far from obvious how to decide HAMPATH in polynomial time. Note that trying all possible paths does not work because there is an exponential number of possibilities. But there is a fast nondeterministic program for it. You guess the path node by node, by choosing a node at each stage that has not already been visited. The time taken is at most quadratic in the number of nodes of the graph. And so HAMPATH is in $\mathcal{NP}$.

What's the most nondeterminism could possibly buy? There is a weak connection between nondeterminism and determinism in the other direction:

Theorem	Let L be a recursive language. If there is a nondeterministic TM for L that runs in time $T(n)$, then there is a deterministic TM for L that runs in time $O(C^{T(n)})$ for some constant C.

Proof	Say L is accepted by NTM N. How many possible configurations of N are there? In the time available, N can use at most $T(n)$ cells on the tape. So, by standard counting, the number of configurations is at most $X = qng^{T(n)}$ where g is the size of the alphabet and q the number of states of N. So, you can proceed as follows.

Generate all possible configurations. Determine which configurations follow which. (This is sometimes called the **configuration graph**.) Then, see if there is a path from the starting configuration to an accepting configuration. The result runs in time polynomial in X, which gives the bound. (Well, actually, you initially get a time bound of $O(X^2)$, which is $O(q^2 n^2 g^{2T(n)})$, but this is $O(C^{T(n)})$ for any $C > g^2$.) ◆

17.5 Certificates and Examples

There is another way to look at nondeterminism. You can certainly program a nondeterministic TM to write a record of all its branching or guessing on a special tape. But you can also get it to write/guess the record at the beginning. In fact, you may think of a nondeterministic decider as a TM that starts by nondeterministically writing an arbitrary string on a special tape called the **certificate tape**. After that, it runs deterministically and the certificate tape is read-only. When the TM has to make a nondeterministic choice, it looks up the next move on the special tape. That is, it does all its guessing at the beginning of the calculation and then works deterministically. This correct "random string" is called the **certificate**.

Example 17.9 The certificate for HAMPATH is the Hamiltonian path. All the program has to do is to check that the edges form a path (end of one is start of next), that the path starts at a and ends at b, and that each node is visited exactly once.

So we have this **prover/verifier** situation. This problem can be decided by a verifier in polynomial time if the verifier is given a hint from an omniscient prover. Note that the correct answer is made: if there is a Hamiltonian path, then the correct hint will be verified and the verifier will say yes; and if there is no Hamiltonian path, then there is no way the verifier can be conned into saying yes.

Although HAMPATH is in $\mathcal{NP}$, its complement does not appear to be so. No simple certificate of the nonexistence of a Hamiltonian path springs to mind. At least in general—the graph being disconnected would be a bit of a giveaway.

Here is an example related to TRUEBF. In dealing with boolean formulas, a **clause** is the *or* of a collection of literals. A formula is said to be in **conjunctive normal form** if it is the *and* of several clauses. A **satisfying assignment** is an assignment of the variables that makes the formula evaluate to TRUE. For example, the formula $x \wedge (x \vee y \vee \bar{z}) \wedge (\bar{x} \vee \bar{y})$ mentioned earlier is in conjunctive normal form and is satisfiable: set x to be TRUE and y and z to be FALSE.

Example 17.10 SAT $= \{ \langle \phi \rangle : \phi$ is a boolean formula in conjunctive normal form that has a satisfying assignment $\}$.

The SAT problem is in $\mathcal{NP}$. The certificate is the assignment of the variables. However, the number of assignments in exponential, so there does not exist an obvious polynomial-time algorithm.

An old problem is to find a fast algorithm that determines if a number is prime or composite, and if composite, determines a factorization. Now, it is important to note that a number m is *input into a program in binary*. Thus, the length of the input is $\log_2 m$. That is, we want algorithms that run in time polynomial in the number of bits, not in time proportional to the number itself. (The latter is easy.)

So, define PRIME as the set of all prime numbers (in binary) and COMPOSITE as the set of all composite numbers. It is clear that COMPOSITE is in $\mathcal{NP}$: simply guess a split into two factors and then verify the split by multiplying the two factors. It is not immediately clear what a certificate for primeness looks like, but elementary number theory provides an answer, and so it has been known for many years that PRIME is in $\mathcal{NP}$.

Then, in 2002 it was shown that PRIME is in $\mathcal{P}$, and hence so is COMPOSITE because $\mathcal{P}$, being deterministic, is closed under complementation. Nevertheless, there is still no polynomial-time algorithm known for determining the factorization of a composite number.

Example 17.11   The SUBSET_SUM problem. Here, you are given as input a collection of numbers in binary and a target in binary. The question is: Is there a subset of the numbers that adds up to the target?

The obvious certificate works: the certificate lists the correct numbers to take (maybe specified as the indices). The checker has only to add the numbers and determine whether their sum is the target.

17.6 $\mathcal{P}$ versus $\mathcal{NP}$

It would seem that $\mathcal{P}$ and $\mathcal{NP}$ might be different sets. However, we do not know. One of the most important unsolved problems in mathematics and computer science today is:

Conjecture $\mathcal{P} \neq \mathcal{NP}$

The Clay Institute offers $1 million for a proof or disproof. (There are easier ways to win a million dollars!)

We can, however, identify problems that are the hardest in $\mathcal{NP}$. These are called the $\mathcal{NP}$-complete problems. They have the property that, if there is a polynomial-time algorithm for any one of them, then there is a polynomial-time algorithm for every problem in $\mathcal{NP}$. They are discussed in Chapter 19.

The question is a two-edged sword: there are numerous $\mathcal{NP}$-complete problems that industry would love to be solvable quickly. On the other hand, almost all of cryptography assumes that the problem of decoding without the secret key is harder than decoding with the secret key, which might not be true if $\mathcal{P}$ equaled $\mathcal{NP}$.

For You to Do!

1. Show that the acceptance problem $A_{nfa} = \{\langle M, w \rangle : M$ is an NFA accepting $w\}$ is in $\mathcal{P}$.

EXERCISES

17.1 Suppose f is $O(n^3)$ and g is $O(n^7)$. What is the order of the functions $f(n) + g(n)$, $f(n)g(n)$, and $f(g(n))$?

17.2 Determine the running time of the TM for $0^n 1^n$ given in Figure 11.1.

17.3 Determine the running time of the TM for unary halving given in Example 12.1.

★ **17.4** **a)** Show that you can "count" in time $n \log n$ on a 1-tape TM. That is, given a string w of symbols, you can compute the binary value of $|w|$ (and leave it next to w, say).

b) Hence, show that you can decide the set E of strings with equal 0's and 1's in $n \log n$ time on a 1-tape TM.

17.5 Consider the language $W = \{ww : w \in \{0, 1\}^*\}$. What is the best time complexity for W on the following models?

a) 1-tape deterministic TM

b) 2-tape deterministic TM

c) 1-tape nondeterministic TM

17.6 Repeat the previous question with the complement of W.

17.7 Discuss and justify the claim that a multitape TM is polynomially related to a computer that has finite internal memory, fixed word length, and fixed instruction set and that can access a bounded amount of external memory at one step.

★ **17.8** Consider the problem of, given a list of numbers, determining if any number appears three or more times. Give a fast algorithm for triplicate detection. (Note: you can do better than $O(n^3)$.)

17.9 **a)** Find a satisfying assignment for the following boolean formula:

$$(x \vee y \vee \bar{z}) \wedge (x \vee \bar{y} \vee z) \wedge (\bar{w} \vee x \vee \bar{y}) \wedge (\bar{w} \vee \bar{x} \vee z)$$

b) Count the number of satisfying assignments.

17.10 Show that $ALL_{DFA} \in \mathcal{P}$. That is, show that you can test in polynomial time whether a DFA accepts every string.

17.11 A 2NFA is a nondeterministic finite automaton with two heads. These heads move independently, both forward and backward, but are constrained to the input portion of the tape, and do not write anything on the tape.

    a) Show that any language accepted by a 2NFA is in $\mathcal{P}$.

    b) Give an example of a language accepted by a 2NFA that is not context-free.

★ **17.12** Show that the set $\mathcal{P}$ is closed under concatenation.

17.13 Show that the set $\mathcal{NP}$ is closed under the star operation.

Ⓗ **17.14** Show that the set $\mathcal{P}$ is closed under the star operation. (Hint: Dynamic programming.)

17.15 Encryption is used to make a message unreadable except by the intended recipient. The typical encryption or decryption of a message entails a polynomial-time process involving the input and a secret key. Explain to your banker why this means that the decryption problem is in $\mathcal{NP}$.

"For You to Do" Exercise Solutions

1. You cannot convert the NFA to a DFA because the DFA can become exponentially large. Instead, you use the idea that motivated the conversion subset construction. Simulate the NFA by keeping track of at each step what states the NFA could be in. Updating this information on the input of a single symbol takes polynomial time.

chapter

18

Space Complexity

$\mathbf{A}$part from time, the other obvious complexity resource is the amount of memory a program uses. There is a fundamental difference between time and space complexity though, in that space can be reused during a computation.

18.1 Deterministic Space

The space used by a TM corresponds to the memory used by a normal computer. When we compute the space used by a TM, we *do not count the input*. So, you may think of the input as being on a **read-only** tape and there being one or more work tapes.

We say that a TM M runs in space $S(n)$ if for all inputs of length n, M uses at most $S(n)$ cells in total on its work tapes.

Example 18.1	The problem SAT can be decided in linear space.

The natural algorithm is to try all assignments. The extra storage required is to keep track of the assignment and to do the verification. Both take at most linear space.

Because it takes one time-step to access one memory cell, the number of memory cells a TM accesses cannot exceed the number of steps for which the machine runs. In particular:

> If a TM runs in time $T(n)$, then it runs in space $T(n)$.

It is very much believed that in general there are languages decidable in space $T(n)$ that are not decidable in time $T(n)$. However, this is not proven in general.

We next show that a polynomial-space machine takes at most exponential time. (And yes, there are certainly programs that take more than exponential time!)

We repeat an observation that we have used before:

Fact	Suppose a deterministic TM runs in $S(n)$ space with g letters in the tape alphabet and q the number of states. If the machine runs for longer than $qng^{S(n)}$ steps on an input of length n, then it is stuck in an infinite loop.

From this we get two consequences. The first is:

Theorem	If a language L is accepted by a TM M running in space $S(n)$ (where $S(n) \geq \log n$), then L is accepted by a TM M' that runs in space $O(S(n))$ but always halts.

Proof	Build a new machine M' that is almost M, but also has a binary counter that counts the number of steps that the machine M has been going. When the counter goes over the previous bound, the machine M' stops and rejects. A counter that has to count up to T takes $O(\log T)$ space. Thus the additional space for the counter is $O(\log(qng^{S(n)})) = O(S(n) + \log n)$. So, M' still runs in $O(S(n))$ space.

♦

The other consequence is:

Theorem	If a language L is decided in space $S(n)$ (where $S(n) \geq \log n$), then there exists a constant C such that L is decided in time $O(C^{S(n)})$.

This theorem does not extend to machines that use less than logarithmic space—indeed, a DFA uses constant space but takes linear time. It turns out that:

Fact	The languages that are decidable in constant space are precisely the regular languages.

The proof of one direction is left as an exercise. We omit the proof that if a language is decidable in constant space, then it is regular.

18.2 Nondeterministic Space

We say that a nondeterministic TM M runs in space $S(n)$ if for any input of length n and for any branch, M uses at most $S(n)$ cells on its work tape. The earlier results about time and space also apply to nondeterministic machines.

Theorem	If a language L is accepted by an NTM M running in space $S(n)$ (where $S(n) \geq \log n$), then L is accepted by an NTM M' that runs in space $O(S(n))$ but always halts.

Theorem	If a language L is decided in space $S(n)$ (where $S(n) \geq \log n$) by a nondeterministic TM, then there exists a constant C such that L is decided in time $O(C^{S(n)})$ by a deterministic one.

The proofs are left as exercises. They use the same ideas as before, but you have to think just a little bit more.

18.3 Polynomial Space

The class $\mathcal{PSPACE}$ is defined as the set of all languages that can be decided in polynomial space. The class $\mathcal{NPSPACE}$ is the set of all languages that can be decided in polynomial space by a nondeterministic machine.

After all the uncertainty about $\mathcal{P}$ and $\mathcal{NP}$, it is perhaps surprising that these two classes are known to be the same.

Savitch's Theorem	$\mathcal{PSPACE} = \mathcal{NPSPACE}$.

Specifically, we show that if there is an NTM for a language L that uses $S(n)$ space (where $S(n) \geq \log n$), then there is a DTM for L that uses $O((S(n))^2)$ space. The theorem follows because the square of a polynomial is still a polynomial. The proof uses recursion.

Proof

Let M be a nondeterministic machine that always halts and runs in space $S(n)$. Then, M runs in at most $T = qng^{S(n)}$ steps for q states and g symbols in the tape alphabet. Now, if necessary, reprogram M to erase the work tape and end in a particular state when it accepts.

As before, a configuration records the contents of the work tape, the state of the machine, and the position of the head on the input tape. To simplify things we pad each configuration to have length $S(n)$. So, there is a unique starting configuration C_s for a given input and a unique accepting configuration C_a. The question is: Is there a legal sequence of moves from C_s to C_a?

Define the boolean function f that takes as arguments two configurations C_1 and C_2 and an integer i such that $f(C_1, C_2, i)$ is TRUE if M can get from C_1 to C_2 in at most i steps and FALSE otherwise. The key is that this function can be computed recursively as follows:

Calculating $f(C_1, C_2, i)$:

```
if i = 1 then return oneStep(M, C₁, C₂)
else {
   for all strings C₃ of length S(n) {
      if f(C₁, C₃, i/2) = TRUE and f(C₃, C₂, i/2) = TRUE
      then return TRUE
   }
   failing which : return FALSE
}
```

The boolean function *oneStep* determines whether configuration C_1 follows from configuration C_2 according to the rules of M.

So, we build a deterministic machine and ask it for the answer to $f(C_s, C_a, T)$. How much storage does this use? The recursive program can use a stack for storage, pushing a "snapshot" of the subroutine's variables each time it calls itself again. Each configuration and hence each snapshot uses $O(S(n))$ space. The maximum number of snapshots on the stack at any one time is $\log T$: at each stage of the recursion, the integer is halved so that the recursion goes down only $\log T$ levels. Because $\log T$ is $O(S(n))$, it follows that the total space needed is $O((S(n))^2)$ cells.

The statement of the theorem now follows.

♦

Example 18.2 A famous example of a problem in $\mathcal{PSPACE}$ is deciding whether an RE generates all strings. This is discussed in the exercises.

It can also be shown that any language given by a context-sensitive grammar is in $\mathcal{PSPACE}$.

 For You to Do! 1. Show that $\mathcal{PSPACE}$ is closed under the star operation.

18.4 Logarithmic Space

We finish this chapter with some more definitions and facts. Maybe one day you can fill in some of the gaps!

> The class $\mathcal{L}$ is the set of problems solvable in $O(\log n)$ space. The class $\mathcal{NL}$ is the set of problems solvable in $O(\log n)$ space by a nondeterministic machine.

Here is an example of a language in $\mathcal{L}$:

Example 18.3 The language $\{\,0^n 1^n : n \geq 0\,\}$ is in $\mathcal{L}$. The key is a counter: a binary counter can be maintained in log space, each increment updating the counter in the obvious fashion. For this language, the work tape counts the 0's and the 1's and compares the counts.

From the earlier result about nondeterministic space and deterministic time, it follows that $\mathcal{NL} \subseteq P$. (The function $C^{\log n}$ is a polynomial in n.) So, it follows that

$$\mathcal{L} \subseteq \mathcal{NL} \subseteq \mathcal{P} \subseteq \mathcal{NP} \subseteq \mathcal{PSPACE} = \mathcal{NPSPACE}$$

Although humanity does not have much of an idea how the space and time classes compare (or at least how to prove such ideas), there are results that show that more space gives us a new language. From this, it follows that

$$\mathcal{L} \neq \mathcal{PSPACE}$$

And that's all that is known about the six classes!

18.1 Give the full proof that a nondeterministic space-bounded machine can be converted into one that always halts.

18.2 Show that the language E of all binary strings with equal 0's and 1's is in $\mathcal{L}$.

18.3 Show that PALINDROMES is in $\mathcal{L}$.

★ **18.4** Show that testing for balanced brackets is in $\mathcal{L}$.

18.5 Show that the acceptance problem $A_{nfa} = \{\, \langle M, w \rangle : M$ is an NFA accepting $w \,\}$ is in $\mathcal{NL}$.

18.6 Show that the acceptance problem $A_{lba} = \{\, \langle M, w \rangle : M$ is an LBA accepting $w \,\}$ is in $\mathcal{PSPACE}$.

18.7 Define ALL_{nfa} as the set of all NFAs that accept every string and NOT_ALL_{nfa} as the set of all NFAs that do not accept every string. Do the same for REs.

    a) Wayne remembered that the acceptance problem A_{nfa} is in $\mathcal{P}$. He then proposed the following algorithm for NOT_ALL_{nfa}: guess a string w that is not in the language and check that w is not accepted. Why does this **not** show that $NOT\_ALL_{nfa} \in \mathcal{NP}$?

    b) Explain why this **does** show that $NOT\_ALL_{nfa} \in \mathcal{NPSPACE}$.

    c) Hence, show that $ALL_{re} \in \mathcal{PSPACE}$.

★ **18.8** Show that if a language is regular, then it can be decided in constant space.

18.9 Show that the set $\mathcal{PSPACE}$ is closed under union.

18.10 Show that the set $\mathcal{NL}$ is closed under both union and the star operation.

"For You to Do" Exercise Solutions

    1. Suppose language A is in $\mathcal{PSPACE}$. We need to build an algorithm for A^*. Assume the input string is w. Then, start by calculating for each substring of w if it is in A. Then, try all possible ways to split w into substrings and see if in any case all the substrings are in A. A split can be encoded by simply an n-bit vector, with a 1 for every point where the string is split. Thus, the extra storage is polynomial.

chapter

19

$\mathcal{NP}$-Completeness

Although the question of whether $\mathcal{P} = \mathcal{NP}$ is unresolved, we can, however, identify problems that are the hardest in $\mathcal{NP}$. These are called the $\mathcal{NP}$-complete problems. They have the property that, if there is a polynomial-time algorithm for any one of them, then there is a polynomial-time algorithm for every problem in $\mathcal{NP}$.

19.1 $\mathcal{NP}$-Complete Problems

The notion of completeness is built on the notion of reduction that was defined in Chapter 15.

A function f (which maps strings into strings) is **polynomial-time computable** if there is a constant k and a TM that computes f in $O(n^k)$ time. A language A is said to be **polynomial-time reducible** to language B if A is reducible to B via a polynomial-time computable function. This is written $A \leq_p B$. The key result is the same as for the original reductions.

Fact
a) If $A \leq_p B$ and B is in $\mathcal{P}$, then A is in $\mathcal{P}$.
b) If $A \leq_p B$ and A is not in $\mathcal{P}$, then B is not in $\mathcal{P}$.

Proof
Suppose the reduction from A to B is given by the function f, which is computable in $O(n^k)$ time. And suppose you can decide membership in B in $O(n^\ell)$ time. Then, build a polynomial-time decider for A as follows. It takes the input w, computes $f(w)$, and then sees if $f(w)$ is in B. But

does the program run in polynomial time? Yes. If w has length n, then the length of $f(w)$ is at most $O(n^k)$ because a program can write only one symbol each step. Then, the test for membership in B takes at most $O(n^{k\ell})$ time. And that's polynomial.

◆

Note that the decider for A might take much much longer than the one for B; however, it is still polynomial in the length of the input.

Definition	A language S is defined to be $\mathcal{NP}$-**complete** if **a)** it is in $\mathcal{NP}$; **b)** for all A in $\mathcal{NP}$ it holds that $A \leq_P S$.

Note that this definition together with the preceding fact means that:

Fact	**a)** If S is $\mathcal{NP}$-complete and S is in $\mathcal{P}$, then $\mathcal{P} = \mathcal{NP}$. **b)** If S is $\mathcal{NP}$-complete and T is in $\mathcal{NP}$ and $S \leq_p T$, then T is $\mathcal{NP}$-complete.

19.2 Examples

There are many, many $\mathcal{NP}$-complete problems. The standard method to proving $\mathcal{NP}$-completeness is to take a problem that is known to be $\mathcal{NP}$-complete and reduce it to your problem. What started the whole process going was the following great idea:

Cook's Theorem	SAT is $\mathcal{NP}$-complete.

We omit the proof of this theorem, also attributed to Levin. The idea is that the computation of a polynomial-time machine can be organized into a polynomial-sized **computation tableau**, one configuration per row. The key insight was to show that you can build a large but polynomial-size boolean formula such that a satisfying assignment of the formula corresponds to an accepting computational tableau.

Here are some examples of $\mathcal{NP}$-complete problems that we saw already. (Proofs of $\mathcal{NP}$-completeness to follow for some of these.) We know that languages and decision problems are equivalent, but in complexity theory it is more common to write them as decision problems.

- ■ HAMPATH is $\mathcal{NP}$-complete.
- ■ SUBSET_SUM is $\mathcal{NP}$-complete.

It is useful to have special cases of SAT that are still $\mathcal{NP}$-complete. One example is:

■ The 3SAT problem is $\mathcal{NP}$-complete:
Input: ϕ a boolean formula in conjunctive normal form with three literals per clause (called 3CNF form).
Question: is there a satisfying assignment?

Several other graph problems are $\mathcal{NP}$-complete. A set of nodes C in a graph is a **clique** if every two nodes in C are joined by an edge. A set of nodes D is a **dominating set** if every other node is adjacent to at least one node in D. A set of nodes V is a **vertex cover** if the removal of V from the graph destroys every edge. (*Vertex* is another word for "node.") For example, in the graph drawn in Figure 19.1, $\{C, H, I\}$ is a clique, $\{A, C, F\}$ is a dominating set, and $\{A, C, E, G, I\}$ is a vertex cover.

The following graph problems are $\mathcal{NP}$-complete:

■ The CLIQUE problem:
Input: graph G and integer k
Question: Does there exist a clique of G of at least k nodes?
■ The DOMINATION problem:
Input: graph G and integer k
Question: Does there exist a dominating set of G of at most k nodes?
■ The VERTEX_COVER problem:
Input: graph G and integer k
Question: Does there exist a vertex cover of G of at most k nodes?

You must be careful of the distinction between parameters that are fixed and input parameters. For example, it is easy to check if a graph

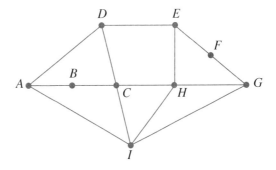

Figure 19.1   An example graph again.

has a dominating set of 1 node. Indeed, for any fixed k, the k-domination problem is in $\mathcal{P}$:

> Input: Graph G
> Question: Is there a dominating set of G of size at most k?

There are n^k possible sets and you have the time to try all possibilities because k is fixed.

19.3　Proving $\mathcal{NP}$-Completeness by Reduction

We do not have to prove that a language is $\mathcal{NP}$-complete using the method of Cook's theorem. Instead, we can use reduction: to prove something is $\mathcal{NP}$-complete, use the earlier fact: *If S is $\mathcal{NP}$-complete, $T \in \mathcal{NP}$, and $S \leq_P T$, then T is $\mathcal{NP}$-complete.*

19.3.1　**3SAT**

We show that 3SAT is $\mathcal{NP}$-complete. The language 3SAT is a **restriction** of SAT; that is, it is the same problem restricted to certain inputs. Because SAT is in $\mathcal{NP}$, it follows that 3SAT is also.

We now show how to reduce SAT to 3SAT. The task is to describe a polynomial-time algorithm for

> *Input:* a boolean formula ϕ in conjunctive normal form
> *Output:* a boolean formula ψ_ϕ in 3CNF form such that ϕ is satisfiable exactly when ψ_ϕ is

The approach is to take each clause C of ϕ and replace it by a family D_C of clauses. For example, suppose there is a clause with five literals; say $C = a \vee b \vee c \vee d \vee e$. What does this mean? This means that, in a satisfying assignment of ϕ, at least one of the five literals must be TRUE. It turns out that you can simulate this by

$$D_C = (a \vee b \vee x) \wedge (\bar{x} \vee c \vee y) \wedge (\bar{y} \vee d \vee e)$$

where x and y are totally new variables. We need to verify two things:

1. If C is FALSE, then D_C is FALSE.
2. If C is TRUE, then we can make D_C TRUE. This will preserve the satisfiability.

To prove Part (1), assume C is FALSE. That is, all of variables a through e are FALSE. To make the first clause of D_C TRUE, we need x to be TRUE.

Then, for the second clause of D_C, we need y to be TRUE. But then the third clause is FALSE, so D_C is FALSE, as required.

To prove Part (2), assume C is TRUE. If a or b is TRUE, then we can set x and y to FALSE; if c is TRUE, then we can set x to TRUE and y to FALSE; and if d or e is TRUE, then we can set x and y to TRUE. It is left to you (*do it!*) to explain how to deal with clauses C of other sizes.

So, this construction yields a boolean formula ψ_ϕ in the right form. If ϕ is satisfiable, then there is an assignment where each clause C is TRUE; this can be extended to make each D_C TRUE. On the other hand, if an assignment evaluates ϕ to FALSE, then one of the clauses, say C', must be FALSE, and thus the corresponding family $D_{C'}$ of clauses in ψ_ϕ is FALSE.

The last thing to check is that the process of conversion can in fact be encoded as a polynomial-time algorithm. It can. That is, we have shown that SAT reduces to 3SAT.

19.3.2 DOMINATION

To show DOMINATION is $\mathcal{NP}$-complete, we must first check that the language is in $\mathcal{NP}$. But that is not hard. The nondeterministic program guesses k nodes and then verifies that they form a dominating set.

We now show how to reduce 3SAT to DOMINATION. That is, we describe a procedure that takes a boolean formula ϕ, and produces a graph G_ϕ and an integer k_ϕ, such that ϕ is satisfiable exactly when there is a dominating set of G_ϕ of k_ϕ nodes.

Suppose input ϕ in conjunctive normal form has c clauses and a total of m variables. For each clause, create a node. For each variable v, create a triangle with one node labeled v and one labeled $\bar{v}$. Then, for each clause, join the clause-node to the three nodes corresponding to the three literals that are in that clause. The result is a graph G_ϕ. For example, the graph for $(x \vee y \vee z) \wedge (\bar{x} \vee y \vee \bar{z})$ is as follows:

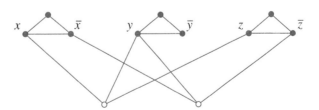

Set $k_\phi = m$. Claim: The mapping ϕ to $\langle G_\phi, k_\phi \rangle$ is the desired reduction.

First of all, the graph can be constructed in polynomial time. Then the main part is to show that the mapping preserves the answer.

If ϕ has a satisfying assignment, then let D be the set of the m nodes corresponding to the TRUE literals in the assignment. Then, each triangle is dominated (there's one node of D in each triangle). And each clause-node is dominated because one of the literals in that clause must be TRUE. So, D is a dominating set of size m.

Conversely, suppose G_ϕ has a dominating set D of size m. Then, D must consist of one node from each triangle because all the unlabeled nodes of the triangles must be dominated. Now, to be dominating, every clause must be connected to one literal in D. So, if you set all the literals corresponding to nodes in D to TRUE, you have a satisfying assignment.

That is, we have shown that `3SAT` reduces to `DOMINATION`.

The preceding reduction illustrates a common pattern. To reduce from `3SAT`, create a "gadget" for each variable and a "gadget" for each clause, and connect them up somehow.

19.3.3 SUBSET SUM

Recall that the input to the Subset sum problem is a set $A = \{a_1, a_2, \dots, a_m\}$ and a target t. The question is whether there is an $A' \subseteq A$ such that the elements in A' sum to t.

We saw already that the problem is in $\mathcal{NP}$. We now show that this problem is $\mathcal{NP}$-complete. This is a reduction from `3SAT`. The previous example suggests the approach to the reduction: define numbers x_i and $\bar{x}_i$ and a target t such that you can take only one of x_i and $\bar{x}_i$, and then some constraint is to be satisfied.

Suppose that we have **vectors** instead of numbers. A vector is just a sequence of values. If two vectors have the same length, then they can be added; the sum of two vectors is the component-wise sum. For example, $(3, 1, 0, 3) + (2, 2, 5, -3) = (5, 3, 5, 0)$. The question now is whether there is a subset whose sum equals a specified vector.

Suppose the input boolean formula ϕ has c clauses and m variables. The vectors will have length $c + m$. For each vector, the first m positions will specify which variable: there is a 1 in the appropriate position and 0 elsewhere. For example, the vector $(0, 1, 0, \cdots, 0; \_\_)$ will be used for the literals x_2 and $\bar{x}_2$. The target vector will be $(1, 1, \cdots, 1; \_\_)$. This will force the selection of exactly one of each variable and its negation.

Now the constraint in `3SAT` is that every clause should be satisfied. That is, you have to choose at least one of the literals in each clause. Thus, the second part of the vector records which clauses each literal is in. For example, if ϕ is

$$(x_2 \vee x_3 \vee \bar{x}_4) \wedge (x_1 \vee \bar{x}_3 \vee x_4) \wedge (x_1 \vee \bar{x}_2 \vee x_4)$$

then the vectors corresponding to the variables are

$$x_1 = (1, 0, 0, 0; 0, 1, 1)$$
$$\bar{x}_1 = (1, 0, 0, 0; 0, 0, 0)$$
$$x_2 = (0, 1, 0, 0; 1, 0, 0)$$
$$\bar{x}_2 = (0, 1, 0, 0; 0, 0, 1)$$
$$x_3 = (0, 0, 1, 0; 1, 0, 0)$$
$$\bar{x}_3 = (0, 0, 1, 0; 0, 1, 0)$$
$$x_4 = (0, 0, 0, 1; 0, 1, 1)$$
$$\bar{x}_4 = (0, 0, 0, 1; 1, 0, 0)$$

Now you would like a target of all 1's. The trouble is that some clauses might have multiple literals chosen. So, define the target as all 1's for the variables and all 3's for the clauses. That is, the target vector is

$$t = (1, 1, 1, 1; 3, 3, 3)$$

Then add what might be called **slack variables**. These are vectors that you can take to round the sum up to the desired target. Specifically, take two copies of each clause:

$$c_1 = (0, 0, 0, 0; 1, 0, 0) \text{ and } c'_1 = (0, 0, 0, 0; 1, 0, 0)$$
$$c_2 = (0, 0, 0, 0; 0, 1, 0) \text{ and } c'_2 = (0, 0, 0, 0; 0, 1, 0)$$
$$c_3 = (0, 0, 0, 0; 0, 0, 1) \text{ and } c'_3 = (0, 0, 0, 0; 0, 0, 1)$$

This allows you to supplement the sum. But to reach 3 in a component, at least one 1 must be supplied by a literal.

That is, we have built a set of vectors and a target vector such that there is a subset of vectors that sum to the target vector exactly when the boolean formula has a satisfying assignment.

Well, actually we do have to argue this both ways. If there is a satisfying assignment, then take the vectors corresponding to the true literals. This produces a vector $(1, 1, 1, 1; \cdots)$ where each entry in the second half is either 1, 2, or 3. Then add c_i and c'_i to taste. And so we have a subset of vectors with the desired property. Going the other way, suppose we have vectors that sum to $(1, 1, 1, 1; 3, 3, 3)$. Clearly, we must have exactly one of x_i and $\bar{x}_i$ for each i. And further, because there are only two slack variables for each clause, the sum of these vectors must sum to at least 1 in each component. That is, the chosen literals hit every clause.

Finally, we go from vectors to numbers. The method is just to think of the vector as the number in decimal. That is:

$$x_1 = 1000011, \bar{x}_1 = 1000000$$
$$x_2 = 0100100, \bar{x}_2 = 0100001$$
$$x_3 = 0010100, \bar{x}_3 = 0010010$$
$$x_4 = 0001011, \bar{x}_4 = 0001100$$

and $t = 1111333$

The only thing to worry about is that we might now be able to reach the target in a way other than that which was intended. But it can be argued that that does not happen. So, we have shown a reduction from 3SAT to SUBSET_SUM.

Believe it or not, these reductions can become routine, eventually.

For You to Do!

1. Show that VERTEX_COVER is $\mathcal{NP}$-complete.
   (Hint: Reduce from 3SAT using two connected nodes for each variable and three connected nodes for each clause.)

EXERCISES

19.1 **a)** Define SPATH as the set of $\langle G, a, b, k \rangle$ such that G is a graph with a path from a to b of length at most k. Show that SPATH is in $\mathcal{P}$.

   b) Define LPATH as the set of $\langle G, a, b, k \rangle$ such that G is a graph with a path from a to b without repeated nodes of length at least k. Show that LPATH is $\mathcal{NP}$-complete. (You may assume the $\mathcal{NP}$-completeness of HAMPATH.)

19.2 **a)** Provide a clause D_C in 3CNF that is satisfiable exactly when $C = a \vee \bar{b} \vee c \vee \bar{d} \vee \bar{e} \vee f$ is true.

   b) Do the same for $C = g \vee \bar{h}$.

Ⓗ **19.3** Show that 2SAT is in $\mathcal{P}$. Hint: Try to find an algorithm for deciding the satisfiability of the *and* of a list of implications; an implication $a \rightarrow b$ means that if a is TRUE then b is TRUE.

★ **19.4** Show that if $\mathcal{P} = \mathcal{NP}$, then there is a polynomial-time algorithm that on input a graph finds a Hamiltonian path if one exists. (Note that $\mathcal{P}$ is only a set of languages!)

19.5 Show that if $\mathcal{P} = \mathcal{NP}$, then there is a polynomial-time algorithm that on input ϕ finds a satisfying assignment if one exists. (Note that $\mathcal{P}$ is only a set of languages!)

19.6 Show that if $\mathcal{P} = \mathcal{NP}$, then every language in $\mathcal{P}$ except $\emptyset$ and Σ^* is $\mathcal{NP}$-complete.

19.7 Show that the CLIQUE problem is $\mathcal{NP}$-complete by reducing from VERTEX_COVER.

★ **19.8** Show that HALF_CLIQUE is $\mathcal{NP}$-complete:
Input: Graph G with m nodes
Question: Does there exist a clique of G of at least $m/2$ nodes?

19.9 Show that HALF_DOMINATING is $\mathcal{NP}$-complete:
Input: Graph G with m nodes
Question: Does there exist a dominating set of G of at most $m/2$ nodes?

19.10 Show that TRIANGLE is in $\mathcal{P}$:
Input: Graph G
Question: Does there exist a clique of G of 3 nodes?

19.11 Is it possible that $\mathcal{P} = \mathcal{NP}$ is undecidable?

★ **19.12** Consider the problem of input a boolean 3CNF formula ϕ, as in 3SAT. Now the question is whether ϕ is a **tautology**, meaning that ϕ is true for *all* assignments of the variables. Show that this problem is in $\mathcal{P}$.

19.13 A *star-free* RE is a regular expression that uses only *or* and concatenation.

    a) Show that there is a polynomial-time algorithm that determines, given a string w and a star-free RE R, if w is in the language of R.

    b) Hence, show that determining if the languages of two star-free RE are different is in $\mathcal{NP}$.

    (H) **c)** Show that the problem is $\mathcal{NP}$-complete by reduction from 3SAT. (Hint: Make the alphabet of your REs be the set of all literals. One RE should generate all possible truth assignments (ordered strings of all true literals). And the other RE should generate all truth assignments that make at least one clause FALSE.)

19.14 A k-**coloring** of a graph is an assignment of one color to each node, using a palette of k colors, such that no two nodes joined by an edge receive the same color. Show that the problem of deciding if a graph has a 2-coloring is in $\mathcal{P}$. (Hint: Try the greedy algorithm.)

Ⓗ **19.15** Show that deciding if a graph has a 3-coloring is $\mathcal{NP}$-complete. (Hint: You might want to use the gadgets pictured below.)

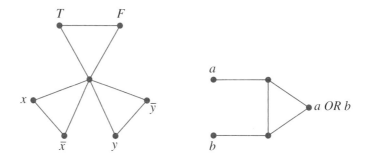

19.16 (TERM PAPER) "The $\mathcal{P}$ vs $\mathcal{NP}$ question is the most important problem in computer science and yet an answer would not change anything." Discuss.

19.17 Convince your instructor that you understood this course.

"For You to Do" Exercise Solutions

1. We first show that **VERTEX_COVER** is in $\mathcal{NP}$. The nondeterministic program guesses k nodes and then checks whether they form a vertex cover.

   We reduce **3SAT** to **VERTEX_COVER**. We describe a procedure to take a boolean formula ϕ, and produce a graph G_ϕ and an integer k_ϕ such that ϕ is satisfiable exactly when there is a vertex cover of G_ϕ of k_ϕ nodes.

   Assume ϕ has c clauses and m variables. For each variable v, create a pair of adjacent nodes with one node labeled v and one labeled $\bar{v}$. For each clause, create three adjacent nodes and join each of these to one of the literals in the clause. The result is a graph G_ϕ that can be constructed in polynomial time. For example, the graph for $(x \vee y \vee z) \wedge (\bar{x} \vee y \vee \bar{z})$ is as follows:

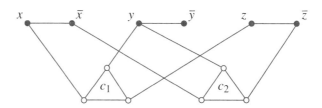

Let $k_\phi = m + 2c$. Claim: the mapping ϕ to $\langle G_\phi, k_\phi \rangle$ is the desired reduction. The main part is to show that the mapping preserves the answer.

Suppose G_ϕ has a vertex cover D of size k_ϕ. Any vertex cover contains at least one node from each node pair and two nodes from each clause triangle. Because D has size $m + 2c$, it follows that this is exactly what D is. Thus, when we remove D, for each clause one node remains, and so the other end of the edge must be in D. That is, the literals in D are a satisfying assignment.

Conversely, suppose ϕ has a satisfying assignment. Then, let D be the set of the m nodes corresponding to the TRUE literals in the assignment. Then, each clause triangle is dominated. So, you can add two nodes from each clause triangle and all edges incident with each clause are taken care of. It follows that G_ϕ has a vertex cover of size $m + 2c$.

That is, we have shown that 3SAT reduces to VERTEX_COVER.

SUMMARY

The time complexity of a TM is the time taken as a function of the input length n in the worst case. The class $\mathcal{P}$ is the set of all languages that are decidable by a TM running in polynomial time. Examples of languages in $\mathcal{P}$ include TRUEBF, PATH, PRIME, and any context-free language.

The class $\mathcal{NP}$ is the set of all languages that are decidable by a nondeterministic TM running in polynomial time. Such a machine is equivalent to a deterministic machine that is handed a certificate to verify the answer.

The space complexity of a TM is the space or memory taken as a function of the input length n in the worst case. The class $\mathcal{PSPACE}$ is the set of all languages that are decidable by a TM running in polynomial space. It is known that $\mathcal{PSPACE} = \mathcal{NPSPACE}$. Examples of languages in $\mathcal{PSPACE}$ include ALL_{re} and any context-sensitive language.

The $\mathcal{NP}$-complete languages are the hardest languages in $\mathcal{NP}$ and every language in $\mathcal{NP}$ polynomially reduces to these. Examples of $\mathcal{NP}$-complete languages include SAT and HAMPATH. A new problem can be proven $\mathcal{NP}$-complete by reduction from a problem already known to be $\mathcal{NP}$-complete.

It is known that $\mathcal{P} \subseteq \mathcal{NP} \subseteq \mathcal{PSPACE}$ and it is believed that there is not equality.

When the problem is known to be NP-complete, or worse, what are you going to do? The best you can hope for is an algorithm that is guaranteed to be close. Alternatively, you can ask for an algorithm that is close most of the time, or maybe is correct but only its average running time is fast. This is in the fields of randomized and approximation algorithms.

*   ***Approximation algorithms** are algorithms that run fast and are guaranteed to be close to the correct answer. For example, a Hamiltonian cycle is a cycle that visits all nodes of a graph exactly once and ends up where it started. In the **traveling salesman problem** TSP, each edge has a weight, and the task is to find the hamiltonian cycle with minimum total weight. Because the HAMPATH problem is NP-complete, it is easy to show/believe that TSP is NP-complete, too. There are numerous approximation algorithms for TSP that guarantee an answer within a certain factor of optimal.*

*   *There are two basic types of randomized algorithms. A **Monte Carlo** algorithm uses randomness and the answer is guaranteed to be correct most of the time. A **Las Vegas** algorithm uses randomness, the answer is guaranteed to be correct, but the running time is only an average.*

*   *We give here only a simple example. Suppose you have two copies of the same long binary file at two different locations: call them F_1 and F_2. Then, a hacker has a go at F_1. You would like to check whether the file is corrupted. Obviously, this can be achieved by sending the one file to the other location. But we would like to minimize the number of bits that are communicated. This can be done with random "check bits."*

*   *Assuming that you have the same random number generator at both ends, you can do the following. Compute a random subset S of the bits by tossing a coin for each bit. Then, compute the XOR of the bits of F_i corresponding to S; call the result c_i (that is, count the number of 1's in the set, and let c_i be the result when this count is divided by 2). Obviously, if F_1 is uncorrupted, then $c_1 = c_2$. It turns out that if $F_1 \neq F_2$, then $c_1 \neq c_2$ 50 percent of the time. So, if you repeat this process 100 times, and the file F_1 is corrupted, there is only a 1 in 2^{100} chance that this won't be noticed. There's more chance of me winning the lottery three weeks in a row!*

References and Further Reading

Aho, A. V., Sethi, R., & Ullman, J. D. (1986). *Compilers: principles, techniques and tools.* Boston, MA: Addison-Wesley.

Althoen, S. C., & Bumcrot, R. J. (1988). *Introduction to discrete mathematics.* Boston, MA: PWS-Kent.

Casti, J. L. (1996). *Five golden rules: Great theories of 20th-century mathematics—and why they matter.* New York, NY: Wiley.

Cohen, D. I. A. (1991). *Introduction to computer theory.* New York, NY: Wiley.

Davis, M. D., Sigal, R., & Weyuker, E. J. (1994). *Computability, complexity, and languages: Fundamentals of theoretical computer science* (2nd ed.). Boston, MA: Academic Press.

Garey, M. R., & Johnson, D. A. (1979). *Computers and intractability: A guide to the theory of NP-completeness.* San Francisco, CA: Freeman.

Hunter, R. (1985). *Compilers: Their design and construction using Pascal.* New York, NY: Wiley.

JFLAP. www.jflap.org

Linz, P. (2006). *An introduction to formal languages and automata* (4th ed.). Sudbury, MA: Jones and Bartlett.

Manna, Z. (1974). *Mathematical theory of computation.* New York, NY: McGraw-Hill.

Martin, J. (2003). *Introduction to languages and the theory of computation* (3rd ed.). New York, NY: McGraw-Hill.

Parsons, T. W. (1992). *Introduction to compiler construction.* New York, NY: Computer Science Press.

Russell, S., & Norvig, P. (2002). *Artificial intelligence: A modern approach.* Upper Saddle River, NJ: Prentice Hall.

Sipser, M. (2006). *Introduction to the theory of computation* (2nd ed.). New York, NY: Thomson.

Sipser, M., Dhagat, A., & Goddard, W. (1989). *Lecture notes for 18:404: Theory of computation*. Cambridge, MA: MIT.

Sudkamp, T. A. (2006). *Languages and machines: An introduction to the theory of computer science* (3rd ed.). Boston, MA: Addison-Wesley.

Wikipedia. www.wikipedia.org

Selected Solutions to Exercises

SOLUTIONS

1.4 (a) 0110 and 00000
  (b) only 1

1.8 All binary strings with at least two 1's.

1.12

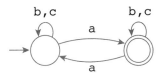

1.16

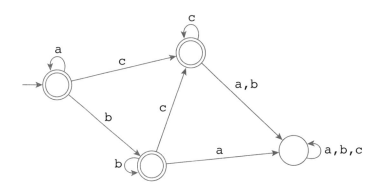

2.4

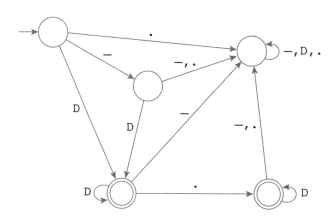

2.8 $0(0+1)(0+1)^*1 + 1(0+1)(0+1)^*0$

2.12 $(00 + 11 + (01 + 10)(00 + 11)^*(01 + 10))^*$

2.16 (a) r^*

    (b) s^*

    (c) $(r+s)^*$

    (d) $(r+s)^*$

3.4

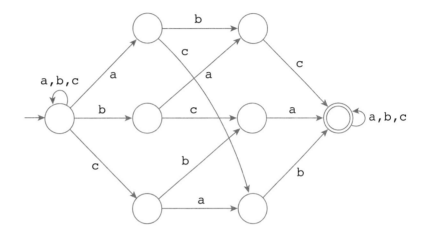

3.8

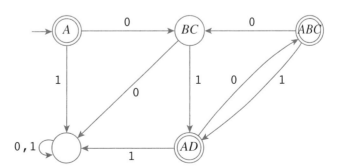

3.12

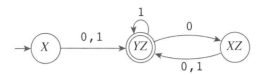

4.4 Take the FA for L and make it into an accept state, every state from which it is possible to reach an accept state.

4.8 Suppose the language L were regular. Let k be the number of states of a DFA for L. Consider the string $z = \mathtt{b}^k \mathtt{a}^{k+1}$—this is in L. Split $z = uvw$ according to the Pumping Lemma. Then, because $|uv| \leq k$, it follows that v is always a string of $\mathtt{b}$'s. Thus, $uv^2w \notin L$, a contradiction of the Pumping Lemma.

4.12 (a) Regular
     (b) Finite and regular
     (c) Regular

4.16 It's given by the RE $\#^m (\#^n)^*$.

6.4 Suppose start variable S_1 generates language L_1 and start variable S_2 generates language L_2. Then, $S \to S_1 \mid S_2$ generates $L_1 \cup L_2$; $S \to S_1 S_2$ generates $L_1 L_2$; and $S \to SS_1 \mid \varepsilon$ generates S_1^*.

6.8 $S \to A\mathtt{10}B\mathtt{01}A \mid \mathtt{0}B\mathtt{01}A \mid A\mathtt{10}B\mathtt{0} \mid \mathtt{0}B\mathtt{0}$
    $A \to \mathtt{0}A \mid \mathtt{1}A \mid \varepsilon$ (any string)
    $B \to \mathtt{0}B\mathtt{0} \mid C$ (starts and ends with equal block of zeroes or starts and ends with 1)
    $C \to \mathtt{1}A\mathtt{1} \mid \mathtt{1}$ (any string starting and ending in 1)

6.12 This was the second practice exercise: all strings of the form $\mathtt{0}^a\mathtt{1}^b\mathtt{0}^c$ such that $a + c = b$.

6.16 (a)

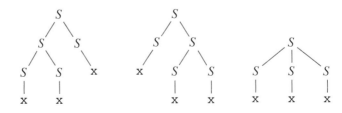

(b) 10. Three trees start with $S \overset{*}{\Longrightarrow} SSS$. For derivation trees that start with $S \overset{*}{\Longrightarrow} SS$ there are three cases: the first S produces x, xx, or xxx. There are 3, 1, and 3 trees, respectively.

6.20 $S \rightarrow SS \mid (S) \mid S^* \mid S + S \mid \text{a} \mid \text{b} \mid \varepsilon \mid "\varepsilon"$

7.4

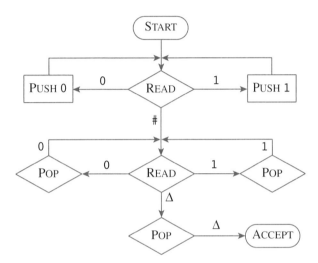

7.8

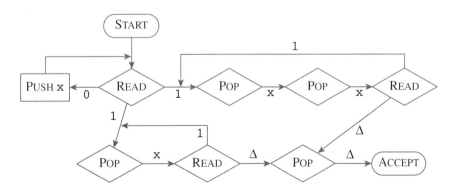

7.12 (a)

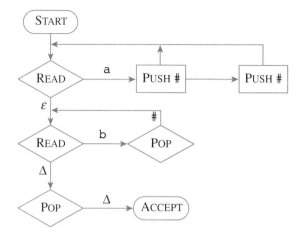

(b)

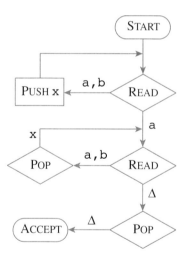

7.16 The PDA reads symbols until it guesses that it is at the start of the first block of 0's. It pushes the block. It then skips symbols until it guesses that it is at the start of the second block. It reads the second block, popping as it goes, and checks that the two blocks have the same length. It then accepts.

8.4 Yes. You can still have multiple ways to produce the same string. For example, $S \to 0A \mid 0B$ with $A \to 1$ and $B \to 1$ has two leftmost derivations for 01. However, if the regular grammar is produced from a DFA by the construction in the text, it is unambiguous.

8.8

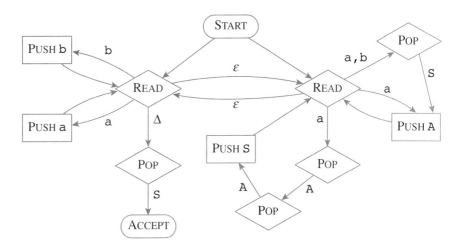

8.12 Initialize all variables as not-usable.
Repeat:
    go through all productions, and if any has right-hand side all entries
        terminals or usable,
    then mark the left-hand side variable as usable;
Until no increase in the set of usable variables.

9.4 Let k be the constant of the Pumping Lemma. Choose the string $z = a^k b^{2k} a^k$; z is in the language. Consider the split of the string z into $uvwxy$. Because vwx combined has length at most k, the string vx cannot contain symbols from all the blocks. This means that $z^{(0)} = uwy$ is not in the language.

9.8 Let C be the complement of the language. A string is in C exactly when at least one of the following conditions is true: (a) the symbols are not in numerical order; (b) the number of 0's does not equal the number of 1's; or (c) the number of 1's does not equal the number of 2's. Each condition can be recognized by a PDA; so C can be recognized by a PDA that guesses which condition to check.

9.12 The non-context-free language $\{\,0^n1^n2^n\,\}$ is the intersection of the context-free languages $\{\,0^n1^n2^m\,\}$ and $\{\,0^m1^n2^n\,\}$.

9.16 The language is not context-free. Let k be the constant of the Pumping Lemma. Choose the string $z = 1^k0^k/1^k0^{k-1}1$. Consider the split of the string z into $uvwxy$. If vx contains only symbols from the denominator, then $z^{(0)}$ is not in the language; if vx contains only symbols from the numerator, then $z^{(2)}$ is not in the language. So, because $|vwx| \le k$, we may assume that v is from the 0's of the numerator and x is from the 1's of the denominator. But then $z^{(0)}$ is not in the language, a contradiction.

9.20 $S \to \mathrm{a}A \mid \mathrm{a}BSSB$
$A \to \mathrm{a}$
$B \to \mathrm{b}$

10.4 0: $[M' \to \cdot\, M],\ [M \to \cdot\, \mathrm{v}(P)]$
1: $[M \to \mathrm{v} \cdot (P)]$
2: $[M' \to M \cdot]$
3: $[P \to \cdot\, P,\mathrm{v}],\ [M \to \mathrm{v}(\ \cdot\ P)],\ [P \to \cdot\, \mathrm{v}]$
4: $[P \to \mathrm{v} \cdot]$
5: $[M \to \mathrm{v}(P\ \cdot\ )],\ [P \to P \cdot\ ,\mathrm{v}]$
6: $[M \to \mathrm{v}(P) \cdot]$
7: $[P \to P,\ \cdot\ \mathrm{v}]$
8: $[P \to P,\mathrm{v} \cdot]$

State	v	(	)	,	Δ	M	P
0	s1					2	
1		s3					
2					acc		
3	s4						5
4			R3	R3			
5			s6	s7			
6					R1		
7	s8						
8			R2	R2			

(b)

Curr state	Stack	To be read	Operation to apply
0		v(v,v)	s1
1	0 v	(v,v)	s3
3	0 v 1 (	v,v)	s4
4	0 v 1 (3 v	,v)	R3
5	0 v 1 (3 P	,v)	s7
7	0 v 1 (3 P 5 ,	v)	s8
8	0 v 1 (3 P 5 , 7 v	)	R2
5	0 v 1 (3 P	)	s6
6	0 v 1 (3 P 5)		R1
2	0 M		acc

10.8

	1	2	3	4	5	6
1	S	.	A	S	A	S
2	.	S	A	S	A	S
3	.	.	A	S	A	S
4	.	.	.	S	A	S
5	.	.	.	.	A	S
6	.	.	.	.	.	S

11.4 Idea: peel off first and last symbols until left with a single 0

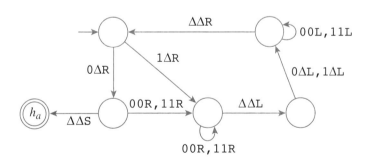

11.8 Idea: find the middle! Idea is to mark first and last symbol and repeat, progressing inward. In this TM, in the first half 0 becomes a and 1 becomes b; in the second half 0 becomes c and 1 becomes d. Accept if the corresponding symbols are different.

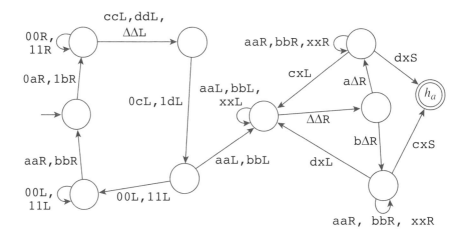

11.12 Idea: Cross off first symbol of every block. Repeat until all symbols are marked. In this TM, 0 becomes x and 1 becomes y.

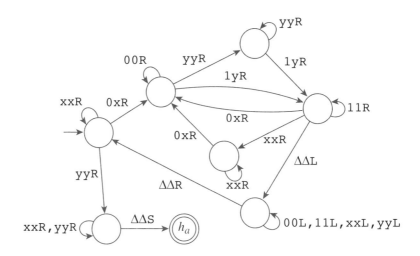

11.16 Place a marker at the right end of the string. Then, repeatedly do the following: find the rightmost uncopied symbol before the marker, mark the symbol as copied, move to the first blank cell after the marker, and write the remembered symbol. At the end, clean up by erasing the original string and the marker.

12.4 (a)

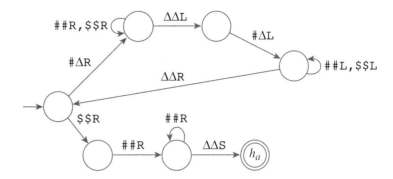

(b)

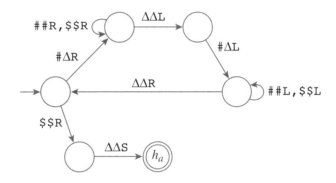

12.8 The key is to write a TM subroutine that will increment or decrement a binary counter. For example, the algorithm for incrementing a binary counter is to start at the right end and repeatedly flip a 1 to a 0 until the first 0 or blank is reached; this is changed to a 1.

12.12 (a) The idea is to go to the right end of the string, and then enter the main routine that remembers the carry (0, 1, or 2) and proceeds right to left.

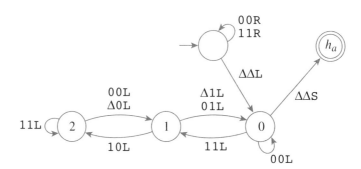

(b) Use the preceding as a subroutine; indeed, the $x \mapsto 3x + 1$ part can be simulated by starting the tripler with a carry of 1. And division by 2 is simply deleting the right-hand zero.

12.16 The NTM guesses where the first tape starts on the second tape. It then compares them symbol for symbol.

12.20 The idea is that for every move left, we shift the entire input one cell to the right. That is, suppose a move left is needed. Then, write on the current cell a marker that this is where the header should be and what the state should be. Then move to the right, moving every value one cell to the right: that is, at each cell record its contents in memory, copy from memory the contents of the previous cell, and go to the next cell. When you reach the end of the used tape, do a left reset. Then, resume the process of moving the contents to the right. Continue until you reach the cell with the special marker; write the contents of the previous cell and go to the recorded state, and continue execution.

12.24 The 2-PDA can simulate the tape by storing the tape in two parts: the portion to the left on one stack and the portion to the right on the second stack. In both cases, the symbol closest to the current position is stored on top of the stack. A move of the tape head transfers a symbol from one stack to the other.

13.4 Say the input RE R has length m. Then, there are finitely many REs of length less than m. Try each in turn, checking if the language of it is the same as the language of R.

13.8 Given TMs M_1 and M_2 for L_1 and L_2, you can run them one after the other (because they both always halt), and then answer if the input string is in $L_1 \cup L_2$ or in $L_1 \cap L_2$.

13.12 If the language L is recursive, then you can compute $\chi_L(w)$ by feeding w into the TM for L and outputting the result. If you can compute χ_L for L with TM N, then you can accept L by taking the input, calculating χ_L, and outputting the result.

13.16 Say r.e. language L is accepted by TM M. A TM for L^* is as follows: On input w, consider all possible ways of breaking up w, and, *in parallel*, run M on every piece. Accept if ever all pieces of a breakup are in L.

13.20 (a) The exact same configuration must recur; there are only this many possible configurations.

(b) On input $\langle M, w \rangle$, calculate the quantity from (a). Then run M on w for this many steps. If M does not halt during this time, then we know it is stuck in an infinite loop and will never accept w.

14.4 Let A be an infinite r.e. set. Let M be a printer-TM for A. Define B as those strings of A that when printed out by M are longer than all previous strings printed out. The language B is infinite because A is infinite. You can decide if w is in B by waiting for the first string to be printed out by M that has length $|w|$ or longer. If this string is w, then accept; otherwise, reject.

15.4 Reduce A_{tm} to this problem. That is, given a TM M and a string w, build a new TM M_w. The TM M_w is programmed to do the following: (1) accept if its input length is even; (2) otherwise, erase its input, (3) write w on the tape, (4) pass it to M, and (5) accept exactly when M accepts.

So, M_w accepts strings of odd length exactly when $\langle M, w \rangle \in A_{tm}$. Hence, if you could answer questions about this problem, you would be able to answer questions about A_{tm}, which we know is undecidable.

15.8 Take G' to be a simple CFG that generates all strings. Then, testing whether G has the same language as G' is equivalent to testing whether G accepts everything, which we know is undecidable (by conversion to a PDA).

15.12 There is only one character. So, each tile can be thought of as a number a_i being the difference in lengths between the upper and lower strings (positive if the upper is longer and negative if the lower is longer). If there is a tile with zero, we are done. If there is a tile with positive and one with negative, then just take the right number of each. The PCP instance has no solution only if the tiles are all positive or all negative.

16.4 Maximum $= x + monus(y, x)$

17.4 (a) You can compute the bits of $|w|$ one at a time: go through w, crossing out every second symbol starting with the first and remembering whether there is an odd or an even number of symbols. This gives the least significant bit of $|w|$, and $|w|/2$ remains. Repeat at most $O(\log n)$ times.

(b) Count the 0's and count the 1's by using the preceding process. Check that they have identical bit patterns.

17.8 Sort the numbers. Then, you can, with a single pass, check to see if a number appears three or more times. This algorithm takes time $O(n \log n)$.

17.12 Suppose languages $A, B \in \mathcal{P}$. For a TM for AB, try all possible ways of splitting the string, sending the first part to the recognizer for A and the second part to the recognizer for B. There are $n+1$ calls to each recognizer, so the overall running time is polynomial.

18.4 Logspace allows you to store a counter. Walk through the input, incrementing the counter for every left bracket and decrementing the counter for every right bracket. The brackets are balanced provided the counter is zero at the end, and never goes negative.

18.8 A regular language can clearly be decided in constant space, in particular the only memory required is the state of the FA.

19.4 Assume there is a Hamiltonian path from a to b. If $\mathcal{P} = \mathcal{NP}$, then there is a polynomial-time subroutine H that tests whether there is a Hamiltonian path between two nodes. Then, you can find the Hamiltonian path from a to b one node at a time. Delete a from the graph. Then, try each neighbor of a; for at least one of them, H must say there is a Hamiltonian path from it to b in what remains; call one such node v_1. Then, delete v_1. Look at its neighbors; again, you can find one for which there is a Hamiltonian path to b. And so on. There are at most $O(n^2)$ calls to H; so the overall running time is polynomial.

19.8 Reduce CLIQUE to HALF_CLIQUE. On input $\langle G, k \rangle$ with G having n nodes we create a graph G':

(i) If $k < n/2$, then form G' by adding $n - 2k$ nodes to G that are adjacent to every node. G' has clique of size $k + (n - 2k) = n - k$ (half its nodes) if and only if G has clique of size k.

(ii) If $k \geq n/2$, then form G' by adding $2k - n$ nodes to G that are adjacent to no node. G' has clique of size k (half its nodes) if and only if G has clique of size k.

19.12 It is very, very hard for a ϕ in 3CNF to be a tautology. This means that every clause is always true. The only way a clause can be always true is that it contains a variable and its complement. So, the test is whether this happens for all clauses.

Glossary

δ The transition function; used in the formal definition of a machine

ε The empty string; has length 0

0^n1^n The language of all strings of 0's followed by an equal number of 1's; not regular

$0^n1^n2^n$ The language of all strings of 0's followed by an equal number of 1's followed by an equal number of 2's; not context-free

2-PDA A PDA with a second stack

2D-FA An FA whose input is a rectangle of symbols

2NFA An NFA with a second head

3SAT The $\mathcal{NP}$-complete language of boolean formulas in conjunctive normal form with three literals per clause

acceptance problem The undecidable problem of determining whether a specified TM accepts a specified string

Ackermann's function A T-computable function that grows faster than any partial recursive function

alphabet A set of symbols

arithmetic progression A sequence of numbers such that the difference between consecutive entries is constant

assignment In a boolean formula, a setting of the values of the variables

A_{tm} The language of representations of TMs M and strings w such that M accepts w

balanced brackets The language of brackets as they would appear in a normal arithmetic expression

boolean formula An expression using the operations *and*, *or*, and *not*, and involving variables that can be either true or false

bounded minimization Defining a new function as the minimum value such that a predicate is true, if there is such a value below a fixed cut-off

Cantor's theorem The subsets of the integers $\mathcal{P}(\mathbb{N})$ is uncountable

certificate A helper string that verifies that the input string is in the language

CFG (context-free grammar) A grammar where every production has a single variable on its left-hand side

Chomsky Normal Form A form of a CFG where every production has right-hand side of either a terminal or two variables

Church's thesis The assertion that there is a TM for a problem if and only if there is an algorithm for a problem

CLIQUE The $\mathcal{NP}$-complete language of graphs that have a clique of a specified size; a clique is a set such that every pair of nodes in the set are joined by an edge

closure Of a set, that the result of some operation acting on the set is always in the set

(complexity) class A set of languages

computation string A record of the computation of a machine on a particular input

configuration A snapshot of a machine including its state and memory

conjunctive normal form A boolean formula that is the *and* of a collection of clauses; each clause is the *or* of some literals

context-sensitive grammar An unrestricted grammar whose productions can be used only if the variable is in a specified context

Cook's theorem The language SAT is $\mathcal{NP}$-complete

countable That a set is finite or can be put into 1–1 correspondence with the natural numbers

counter automaton An FA whose only extra memory is a counter

derivation tree The derivation of a string from a CFG drawn as a tree

diagonalization A technique that produces a string, not in a list, by taking the diagonal and altering each symbol

distinguishable strings There exists a suffix such that the addition of the suffix to one string is in the language and to the other string is not

DNA computing Using DNA to represent data and compute with it

DOMINATION The $\mathcal{NP}$-complete language of graphs that have a dominating set at most a specified size; a dominating set is such that every other node is adjacent to some node of the set

FA (finite automaton) A model of computation whose memory is a fixed set of states

FIRST set In a CFG, the terminals that can appear at the start of a string derived from a specific variable

FOLLOW set In a CFG, the terminals that can appear following a specific variable in a derivation

formal definition Expressing a machine or mechanism as a mathematical object

function A mapping associating a (not necessarily distinct) element of the range to each element of the domain

Goldbach's conjecture The unproven claim that every even number at least 4 is the sum of two primes

graph A set of nodes some pairs of which are connected by edges

Greibach Normal Form A specific form of a CFG

halting problem The undecidable problem of determining whether a specified TM halts when processing a specified string

HAMPATH The $\mathcal{NP}$-complete problem of determining whether a graph has a Hamiltonian path; a Hamiltonian path is one that visits every node exactly once

item-set A collection of LR(0)-items

JFLAP Software that you can use to draw and manipulate machines and representations

Kleene's theorem The following are equivalent for a language: there is a DFA for it, there is an NFA for it, there is an RE for it

$\mathcal{L}$ The class of languages decidable in $O(\log n)$ space

language A set of strings

LBA (linearly bounded automaton) A TM that is restricted to $O(n)$ space

leftmost derivation A derivation where the leftmost variable is replaced at each step

lexical analysis Identifying the basic syntactical parts of a program

librarian paradox A conundrum mentioned in this book

linear grammar A CFG where every right-hand side has at most one variable

literal In a boolean formula, a variable or its negation

LR(0)-item A production with a position marked on the right-hand side; used in constructing a shift–reduce parser

LR(1) grammar A CFG where looking one symbol ahead is enough to decide whether to shift or reduce

monus A version of subtraction where negative numbers are converted to zero

NFA (nondeterministic finite automaton) An FA that is allowed multiple transitions for the same input symbol as well as ε-transitions

$\mathcal{NL}$ The class of languages decidable in $O(\log n)$ space by a nondeterministic machine

nondeterminism Having multiple next moves; a string is accepted exactly when there exists some sequence of moves that ends up in an accept state

$\mathcal{NP}$ The class of languages decidable in polynomial time by a nondeterministic machine

$\mathcal{NP}$**-complete** A problem that is the hardest of all problems in $\mathcal{NP}$; believed to not be in $\mathcal{P}$

nullable variable In a CFG, a variable that can generate the empty string

order of a function The growth of a function ignoring constants; expressed in O-notation

$\mathcal{P}$ The class of languages decidable in polynomial time

palindrome A string that reads the same backward as forward

parsing Determining whether a string is generated by a CFG, and if so, determining its derivation tree

PCP (Post's correspondence problem) The undecidable problem of choosing an ordering of tiles such that the overall top and bottom strings are the same

PDA (pushdown automaton) An NFA whose extra storage is a stack

primality testing The problem of determining if a number is prime

primitive recursive function A function defined from the zero, successor, and projection functions using composition and primitive recursion

printer-TM A TM with no input but that prints its language on its output tape

proof by simulation Establishing the equivalence of two models by showing how to emulate one with the other

proving $\mathcal{NP}$-completeness by reduction A technique of showing a problem is $\mathcal{NP}$-complete by reducing another $\mathcal{NP}$-complete problem to it

$\mathcal{PSPACE}$ The class of languages decidable in polynomial space

Pumping Lemma The lemma giving a property of regular or context-free languages whose contradiction proves that a given language is not of that type

quantum computing A possible method of computation using quantum states to store data

queue automaton An FA whose extra storage is a queue

RE (regular expression) A description of a regular language using the operations union, concatenation, and star

r.e. language (recursively enumerable language) A language that is recognized by some TM

recursive language A language that is recognized by some TM that always halts

reduction A function that maps strings to strings while preserving whether the string is or is not in a specified language

regular grammar A CFG for a regular language where every right-hand side is either a terminal or a terminal followed by a variable

SAT The $\mathcal{NP}$-complete language of boolean formulas in conjunctive normal form

Savitch's theorem A nondeterministic TM can be converted to a deterministic TM that uses the square of the space of the original

self-denying TM The language of descriptions of TMs that do not accept their own description

self-reference This entry

space complexity The order of the amount of memory used by a (best) TM

stack A storage mechanism that is last-in, first-out

state The internal memory of an FA

statechart A depiction of the functioning of an object; similar to an FA diagram

string A sequence of symbols

string processing Answering questions about strings

SUBSET_SUM The $\mathcal{NP}$-complete problem of determining, given a set of numbers in binary and a target, is there a subset of the numbers that sum to the target

time complexity The order of the amount of time used by a (best) TM

TM (Turing machine) A model of a computer obtained by taking an FA and giving it an infinite tape where it can read and write symbols

transducer A TM that produces a specific output string

unary language Any language whose alphabet has only one symbol

unbounded minimization Defining a new function as the minimum value such that a predicate is true

unrestricted grammar A grammar whose productions allow strings to be replaced by strings

usable variable In a CFG, a variable that generates at least one string of terminals

Index